Amazon Emotions

D1473004

2nd edition, revised and enlarged

Francisco Ritta Bernardino

Photographs by Leonide Principe

Amazon Emotions

2nd edition, revised and enlarged

A Sentimental-Photographic Guide
to the Amazon Ecosystems

photoamazonica
.com

Published by:

photoamazonica Editora
Caixa Postal 231
69011-970 - Manaus Amazonas Brazil
E-mail: emotions@photoamazonica.com
Website: http://www.photoamazonica.com
Phone: (092) 656-3348   fax: (092) 656-4547

1st edition: 1996 in Portuguese and English
2nd edition: 1998 revised and enlarged, in Portuguese, English, and Spanish
Layout and Advisory Services: Álvaro Marques – Paper Comunicação
Copy editing: Alcides Werk
English Translation by Doris Ethel Hefti

Sponsored by:

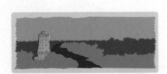

Ariaú Amazon Towers

Rua Silva Ramos, 42 - Manaus Amazonas Brazil
Phone: (092) 800-5000 / 622-5000 fax: 233-5615
E-mail: treetop@internext.com.br
Website: http://www.amazontowers.com

B518

Bernardino, Francisco Ritta, Principe, Leonide.
Amazon Emotions: A Sentimental-Photographic Guide to the Amazon Ecosystems / Francisco Ritta Bernardino, Photos by Leonide Principe. English Translation by Doris Ethel Hefti / Manaus: PhotoAmazonica Editora, 1998.
224 p. photographs.
ISBN 85-87074-01-6 (Portuguese ed.)
ISBN 85-87074-02-4 (English ed.)
ISBN 85-87074-03-2 (Spanish ed.)

1. Ecosystems - Amazon. 2. Amazon - Ecosystems. I. Bernardino, Francisco Ritta. II. Principe, Leonide. III. Hefti, Doris Ethel, transl. IV. Title.

CDD: 574.5(811)

Mating of butterflies of the *Methona* genus.

To ease reading for those unfamiliar with the Amazon realm, in this second edition we have included a glossary of terms common to inhabitants of the region (*caboclos**). All words followed by an asterisk (*) will be found in the glossary in alphabetical order.

The cover was designed with computer graphics resources.

Summary

Acknowledgments 8
Preface 10
THE GREEN – Poem by Alcides Werk 13
Foreword 16
Presentation by F. Ritta Bernardino 19
Presentation by Leonide Principe 23

Introduction 27
The Great Mother 28
Is this destruction irreversible? 30

Landscapes 37
The Amazon Plains 39
"The river controls life" 51

Plant and Animal Life 57
The Wise Gardener 59
The Kingdom of Biodiversity 66
U-iara, the *boto vermelho** 106

Indians and *Caboclos* 123
Walahari-á 124
Experiencing Nature 134
People of the Backlands 147
*Ribeirinhos** 150
*Seringueiros** 161

The Future 167
An Amazon Civilization 168
A Great Challenge 180

Epilogue 189
Glossary 212

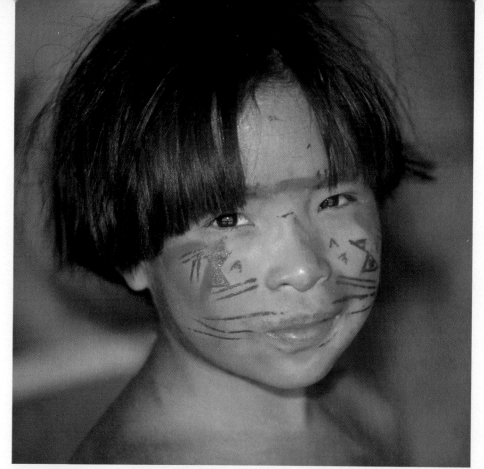

Boy of the Makiritari
ethnic group of
Indians living in Brazil
and Venezuela. Their
language is called
Yekuana, and in
Brazil they are known
as *Maiongong.*

Island on the Negro River
near Barcelos. White
sand banks appear in the
bed of the river in the
periods between the high
and low water
(*vazante**) seasons.

Acknowledgements

To Rosa, Ritta Junior, Edilson, Edson, Ellen, Eliane and Luiz Felipe,

Iara, Carlo, Luna, Claudio, *mamy* Olga, *nonno* Carlo, and *mestre* Gabriel.

Caboclo* lullaby. Woman with baby black-capped capuchin (*Cebus apella*).

Paper, the raw material of this book, is made from trees. Reverent thanks is due to Nature and to all those who bear this in mind when handling a book... and plant a tree...

...we also extend thanks to all those who have supported and encouraged us to increasingly direct our actions toward environmental conservation. Our thanks cover the scope that ranges from the anonymous *caboclos** living in the vastness of the Amazon planet, to illustrious personages such as oceanographer Jean-Jacques Cousteau who inspired us during his expedition to the Amazon aboard the Calypso. We also thank those who honored us by staying at the Ariaú Amazon Towers: Governor Amazonino Mendes, Senator Bernardo Cabral, Senator Gilberto Mestrinho, Chancellor Helmut Kohl, President Koivisto of Finland, Count Pirelli, the Duke of Kent, labor union leader Luís Inácio Lula da Silva, President Roman Herzog of Germany, Norwegian Prime Minister Gro Brudtland, Jimmy Carter, Bill Gates, Jacques Villeneuve, Roman Polanski, Emanuelle, Romário, Olivia Newton John, and many others, perhaps less well known, but no less encouraging.

Preface

Orchid (*Acacallis cyanea*). The flowers of this species often feature a bluish color, and the plant can be considered rare as it is very sensitive to environmental conditions. It is very difficult to grow outside of its natural habitat and is highly valued on the orchid-growing market. It is found mainly in *igapó** vegetation and in lowland forests near *igarapés**. In *igapó** vegetation, where it is more frequently found, it often remains underwater for 2 or 3 months. European botanists on excursions through the Amazon in the early 1900s were fascinated by this orchid's beauty.

Whether we like to admit it or not, the Amazon region, from the viewpoint of conventional geopolitical concepts, is more than an exclusive and prized Brazilian possession. It is an agonizing world's hope for quality, and as such, the prized possession of all humanity.

Inhabitants of the Amazon region suddenly perceived the spirit of preservation as more than a duty – as a right. The explanation: communication. Radio, newspapers, and television have shown how the planet is being degraded, and how quickly this degradation occurs. Thus, by a process of natural inference, inhabitants of the region feel the need to preserve what they know to be incomparably rich and beautiful.

Ecological tourism is one of the wisest means these inhabitants have discovered to preserve their paradise. The Ariaú Towers is an eloquent example of this statement. It's owner and mastermind, imbued with this feeling, crossed the borders of the Western world and ventured on into the East by receiving at the hotel people of the most diverse origins, allowing them to feel true and direct contact with the jungle and all its exuberant beauty. After their stays at the hotel, personages well-known in the world of politics from many countries, Hollywood actors, VIPs, and young people leave their expressions of undying love of the Amazon, their fascination with the unique pleasure of being in the forest, registered in the hotel's guest book.

Amazonino Armando Mendes
Governor of the State of Amazonas

THE GREEN (VERDE)

Alcides Werk

There is a green dream in your soul
that fulfills its role
with life.

There is a magic power in your hands
that acknowledges earth's bounty
and puts down roots.

There is a miracle in your love
that bears flower and fruit
and perpetuates itself.

There can be no success
for those who build deserts
and hunger
as long as we can repeat,
in each generation,
the simple gesture of your clean hands
and of your word,
for love of the green.

TRILHA D'ÁGUA - Poesia Reunida
4th Edition - Manaus, 1994

Photo: Mariuá archipelago — Negro River,
in Barcelos County.

Red macaws (*Ara macao*) — Ever faithful, macaws choose one sole companion for life. The consorts are very assiduous in their courtship, arranging one-another's feathers and caressing one-another. The male regurgitates food for the female, courting her

and strutting in front of her with his tail spread... Should one of
the couple have a fatal accident, the other may commit suicide
by soaring up to a great height and then closing its wings to
plummet to earth.

Roraima plains (or *lavrado*, as it is known to the natives).

Foreword

Roraima formation: on a flight from Maturacá to the Pico da Neblina.

The original title of this book was "Amazon Emotions – A Sentimental-Photographic Guide to the Amazon Ecosystem". This was because we were focusing only on the better-known image of the Amazon region as one of forests and rivers. However, in view of new expeditions, interviews with researchers, and the enormous volume of bibliographic material on the subject – very rewarding experiences – we decided to change "ecosystem" to the plural, thus, "Amazon Emotions – A Sentimental-Photographic Guide to the Amazon Ecosystems".

At first glance, this may seem to be a very slight difference. However, the range of knowledge we acquired by means of practical and ongoing experience with this immense and mysterious Amazon world, and included in the book, justifies this change.

What had seemed to be a continuous and uniform forest canopy proved to be extremely varied and unpredictable. We found mountains, savannas, plains, dunes, and many other

variations classified in 112 ecosystems. In each of these ecosystems, the organization of life takes on specific characteristics: open forest, dense forest, with few lianas, with a lot of lianas, and so on.

In fact, this knowledge is merely a starting point for a fabulous journey we attempted to portray, illustrating it as far as possible, with photos that represent a myriad of other windows opened to the extremely varied and surprising Amazon landscapes.

We have presented this information as simply as possible to make reading more enjoyable. Readers will note that we attempted to make images the message's main vehicle, and to uphold an excellent level of graphic quality capable of reproducing the original photos with the utmost fidelity.

While it is true that images may establish the photographer's view

Igapô* – A stretch of forest with its own particular vegetation where water penetrates regularly during floods.

Dunes near the Serra do Aracá in Barcelos County – Negro River.

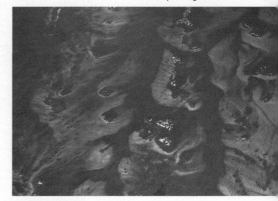

of reality, they cannot establish reality itself. Reality will always be there in its place.

Actual physical participation is essential if we are to achieve true contact – spectators must see things through their own eyes. One must be present for the senses to capture the feelings, with all the refinement of nature's colors and aromas, allowing the mind and the heart to truly assimilate the feeling of being in the wild.

Serra dos Surucus – Roraima State, in the Yanomami Indian Reservation.

Ariaú Amazon Towers:
elevated walkways.

Presentation
by Francisco Ritta Bernardino

When I accompanied Chancellor Helmut Kohl on a visit to the home a *ribeirinho**, I perceived the vital importance of being acquainted with the Amazon reality at the highest levels of political power where decisions are made that ultimately affect the future of humanity. I am certain that the Chancellor left the Amazon with ideas quite dif-

Francisco Ritta Bernardino, co-author of this book, and designer and owner of the Ariaú Amazon Towers.

ferent from those he had upon his arrival. He not only confirmed this, but also demonstrated his effort to capture the essence of an environment as special as that of the Amazon. This very real interest he evidenced will certainly

19

Dawn on Arara Lake – on the left bank of the Negro River.

help him, and help us, in political debates that feature the Amazon region.

It is my opinion that interpretation of the Amazon reality, as it has been carried out to date, has been dangerously deformed due to the lack of practical living experience. The true Amazon is forgotten in the jungle while public opinion is formed by easily sold journalistic sensationalism that limits itself to burning off in the region, a cataclysmic vision that gives the impression that we are nearing the apocalypse. These subjects end up forming the basis of discussion at high levels, often featuring an abstract and ingenuous comprehension. This sort of discussion definitely does nothing to further preservation of the Amazon. Before talking and judging, the Amazon must be seen and experienced. Only then will people perceive that the problem is not merely one of a burnt off forest, but also, among other things:

a) the urgent need of an economic alternative capable of attracting investment, and at the same time, of redeeming the dignity of those who inhabit the backlands of the Amazon region;

At the Ariaú Amazon Towers – the World Peace Tower symbolizes the love and brotherhood that should reign among all the people on Earth.

b) development of research and conservation projects not restricted to the government level, by foundations and associations truly interested in environmental issues.

Issues related to the Amazon cannot be resolved from the outside. Solutions must stem primarily from the inhabitants themselves, with generous support of all those who truly desire an ever green Amazon.

When I was a sergeant in the army, an expedition was organized that covered sixty kilometers between the headwaters of the Apuaú and Cuieiras Rivers. The young and enthusiastic officer who led the mission was certain that we would cover this distance in four days, and ordered us to carry the amount of food corresponding to his calculations. Based on my own experience, I defended the opinion that we would take at least twelve days to cover that distance. However, I only managed to get our rations increased to cover an additional two days. We set out, following the direction our compass indicated. On the sixth day we were still very far from our destination and had run out of food. In order to survive, we were forced to eat leaves, roots, and wild animals – even snakes – and we only reached our destination on the twelfth day.

Reckless disregard for the Amazon reality is historic, and has already defeated magnates such as Daniel Ludwig who lost close to a billion dollars on the Jari project, or Henry Ford who witnessed the collapse of his dream of supplying the world with rubber made of the raw material produced at Fordlândia, his rubber plantation.

Nightfall at the Furo do Meio. This *furo** links the Ariaú *paraná** with the Negro River near the Ariaú Amazon Towers.

It is therefore my opinion that solutions for the Amazon problem must come from within the forest. The solutions cannot be pre-fabricated or canned in the centers (forums) of political power. We must listen, very attentively and humbly, to those who inhabit the region: the age old wisdom of the Indians; the experience of generations of *caboclos**; and the not always easy attempts at adjustment of those dedicated to research and to development in harmony with nature.

*Paraná** that empties into the Solimões River.

Presentation
by Leonide Principe

The wind and currents make navigating
from Fortaleza in Brazil, to Cayenne in French
Guiana, a very pleasant cruise. This is especially true of sailboats that can cover as much as
200 miles a day with tail winds. When I made
this trip in 1988, the only precaution I took as
captain was to keep a safe distance – at least
100 miles – from the coast when we neared the
mouth of the Amazon River. This river mouth
is 320 kilometers wide, with enormous islands
such as Marajó which measures 48,000 square
kilometers, an area the size of Switzerland.

Even allowing such a large margin of safety,
the great river shows signs of its size: the water
changes color and it is not uncommon to find
tree trunks carried by the ocean's waves. This
is not surprising if we keep in mind that the

The *boto vermelho**
(*Inia geoffrensis*) in the
Ariaú *paraná**.
As the *ribeirinhos** say:
it's floating. People of
the interior believe that
washing one's face
with the water left by
the wake of the *boto*
will cure any disease in
this part of the body.

river constitutes one-fifth of all the fresh water
on the planet. For two days, I felt the giant's
venerable presence. I was able to imagine what
Spanish navigator Vicente Yañez Pinzón must
have felt in the year 1500 when he realized that
although he was so far from the coast of the
"New World", he was sailing in fresh water.

During the long hours at the helm, my mind
tried to penetrate the fascinating geography of
the mythical Amazon: my imagination flowed
freely over the water's heavy surface. When, in
the vision of my dream, I perceived land on the
sides, I was already at the mouth of the river, a
new world to me. I wandered up further and
further, seeking the origin of all that. My fantasy took wing – a fast, low flight full of curves.
All along the course of the great river, with no

difficulty in identifying the majestic main stream, I carried on past the countless tributaries all the way to the foot of the mountain range.

Several thousands of years ago there was no Amazon River. Some thousands of years later, the region where the Andes are currently located emerged abruptly, creating a barrier for the waters and forming a huge inland lake. Thus, upon reaching this same barrier, I interrupted my imaginary flight, returning to the salt-laden ocean breeze that roused me from my dream. I continued my ocean voyage with nostalgic memories of the river and a promise to return. It was a promise that remained hidden, like a stowaway, aboard the boat.

Initial view of *Ilha Comprida* in the Anavilhanas archipelago. This group of islands and the Mariuá archipelago further downstream in the Negro River are said to be the largest river archipelagos in the world.

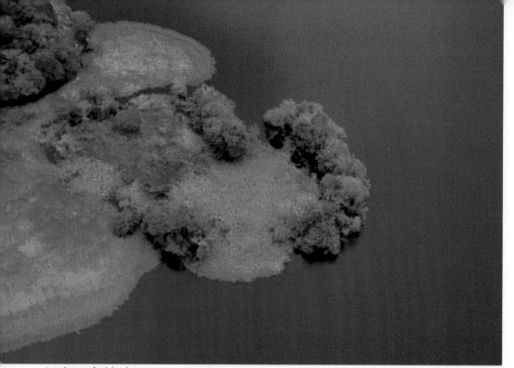

Aerial view of a lake during high water season in the region of the Ariaú *parana**.

Aerial view of a stretch of the Jaú River.

The muddy-colored water was left behind and the ocean completely recovered its customary deep blue tone. After several days of sailing I reached my destination – the islands of the Caribbean – leaving behind my thoughts of the Amazon River. But way down there in the depths of my subconscious, that stowaway idea that had boarded at the mouth of the river came out of hiding again. Four months later, on a flight from Barbados to Manaus, I was glued to the window of the airplane on my way to an appointment at the INPA*.

There I met with Vera M. F. da Silva, a researcher at the Laboratory of Aquatic Mammals, and set up the parameters for what was to sprout roots and anchor me to the region... roots that began with my first photo-journalistic report on the *boto vermelho**...

When the wind dies down, forest spirits are
reflected in the mirror-like waters of the *igapós**.

Introduction

The Great Mother

Information about the Amazon has already spread throughout the world. However, current ideas regarding the situation of the tropical forest encountered in this region must be reformulated. The media addresses this issue from various angles, and the views set forth are not always correct. We want to contest one of these opinions currently prevalent among the many being widely aired: that the Amazon is being irredeemably destroyed.

We must acknowledge that in southern Pará State and in Rondônia man is leaving the mark of destruction. The area of the Amazon region devastated over the past thirty years is already the size of France.

However, there are those who imagine that the Amazon has turned into an enormous bonfire, and who consider even the smoke of a *caboclo*'s* small *roçado** to be part of the great disaster. In fact, these people are unaware of the vastness of the Amazon region. Although danger does exist and man's ambition is extremely aggressive, the immensity of the spaces and the difficulty of absolute and unlimited control over the Amazonian nature are factors that continue to make it possible to preserve its integrity.

Modern technology has to deal with the natural resistance of this region: machines made to open up roads through the region's sandy or swampy terrain become prisoners of bogs and rust. Difficult access is the Amazon forest's most efficient defense – the main reason why we can still boast one of the last, and the largest, truly wild areas on the planet.

Samambaia (fern) – A plant commonly grown in vases because of the beauty of its leaves. It is not very demanding in terms of nutrients and is frequently found in areas that feature damp, sandy, acid soil. The photos show an adult plant and a new shoot beginning to open.

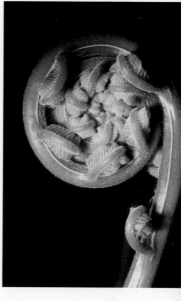

Is this destruction irreversible?

Navigating the Negro River one day in the company of my friend Victor Py-Daniel (a researcher at INPA*), we were talking about the volume of water that flows through the Amazon basin when we suddenly noticed he had assumed a very serious expression, as though something were threatening us.

He exclaimed: "Today we are cruising on the Negro River certain that our boat will not run aground on a sand bank. Araújo, our captain, knows the river as did his father before him, and he knows that during the dry period there is a channel to navigate and it remains continually navigable, as always, under such conditions. But... it could be that one day, maybe even in the near future, we will no longer be able to navigate as we are doing today, simply because there will no longer be that half-meter of water that's sufficient for the shallow draft of our boat...

...Although we don't want this to happen, it's part of the ongoing change in our Universe...

Victor is originally from the state of Rio Grande do Sul. He has been living in the Amazon for twenty years carrying out extensive field research in regions where hardship and risk are part of his daily routine. He is confident that he is doing his part (scientific) to hamper the degenerative process that attacks Amazônia from all sides and in all forms, even the most camouflaged such as indifference and the aloofness of the human bureaucratic machine.

"But Victor" we asked, "what makes you say that?" Our blood would certainly have frozen in our veins were it not for the temperature (40° C).

*Garimpo** on the Pico da Neblina.

"How could there possibly be an Amazônia without water, when we know that the region currently accounts for one-fifth of all the fresh water on this planet? Where would all this water go? You must be joking!"

Our researcher became much more serious than usual. "No, I'm not joking!" A feeling of anguish seemed to settle on us... Wouldn't it be more worthwhile to believe in the power of positive thinking, to show that there is still something left to save?

Our Amazon castle seemed to be crumbling into ruin, right there before our eyes: the springs of the rivers overturned by miners sluicing and panning in their search for gold; tons of mercury poisoning the water that the miners themselves use for cooking and drinking; river banks crumbling because farmers clear the land right up to the river's edge; fish becoming scarce due to lack of food (seeds and fruit) due to the removal of trees that previously lined the river banks and the planting of *várzeas** and *igapós**.

The *garimpeiros**, loggers, farmers – all intent on their own tasks – and thereby transforming the ecological balance. It seems that Victor is right. And what if the waters disappear tomorrow, or the day after, or in the next century?

"Victor, is this destruction really irreversible?" we asked again. It was as though we were trying to climb up the red banks along the margins of the rivers to replace the fallen trees. "Do you think we will be able to revert all this contamination?"

"The irreversibility" Victor went on "began with construction of the first forts put up by the Spaniards, English, French, and Portuguese. Amazônia is one of the three last large uninhabited areas of the world, perhaps the only one that could be readily habitable. But, ecologically speaking, the economic model being applied to this occupation is incompatible with human integration. Use of the land, with no commitment to ecology, is standard operating procedure in Amazônia, and always has been. The idea of extracting from the world all of its potentialities until they are depleted and with no thought of preservation is the same, although the perpetrators are no longer the Portuguese of the age of conquests... Only the means have changed: colonization is now carried out by means of technology. In other words, possession of the process of knowledge and its application. The groups most strongly armed with information about ecology and the political power to implement their proposals are in the countries that apply, by means of technology and/or political-economic maneuvers, an attitude of headlong exploration of the natural resources to continue to uphold their 'modus vivendi' – a feature common to nearly all human cultures.

Gold nuggets extracted from a *garimpo** on the Pico da Neblina.

Different peoples have different levels and types of knowledge, and it is these that continue to determine their "differentness": occupiers / occupied. There is no humanitarianism to be found in the name of joining forces to take advantage of natural resources. In the process of colonization, colonizers promoted cultural destructuring of the peoples they dominated, and the consequences of this destructuring have been felt throughout time, regardless of the culture. This is the case of cutting-edge technology and the development of top quality research centers. Only access to technological knowledge can generate a posture of joint development featuring proper handling of natural resources and improved quality of life. Instead of 'Pure Ecology' contaminated by the myth of 'Paradise Lost', what we need is technology and economic structure in conjunction with fraternity aimed to promote the development of 'humane' peoples (respecting all their diversities) who need, and will continue to need a place to live".

We are all feeling a sense of relief. A tenuous thread of hope that fueled the will to carry on gradually replaced the apocalyptic image. It was necessary to have faith. The fog that had obscured our minds, confusing our thoughts, was slowly dissipated by the beginnings of a light breeze. It deposited on the deck of the boat so many projects and ideas that had up to then been struggling to eliminate the gray clouds that still hover over the Amazon due to man's boundless ambition to acquire goods/positions. It is normal for humankind to stubbornly become fixed on the apparent effects of problems and fail to perceive the causes of these problems. We are all liable to get caught in this trap.

It's no use to try to prevent *caboclos** from burning off their manioc fields to prepare them for new planting, nor is it any use to set up police operations to hunt down ambitious *garimpeiros**. At the root of these situations is a political and economic problem that must be analyzed and solved on the social level. We have no right to prohibit hungry people from eating monkeys or turtles, or to forbid that they trade animal hides for their basic survival. Hunger, poverty, the natural instinct for survival will always prevail.

Likewise, it is no use to tell miners that mercury is harmful to their health and that the rivers must not undergo artificial erosion. One of the major causes of the existing devastation is speculation on the part of powerful financial groups in the main centers of international power. Devastation of the Amazon also stems from the vast and well-decorated offices of economic and political leaders, precisely those places where the destiny of nations and peoples are defined. These same powers will soon be making decisions that will affect the whole planet...

...the destruction is reversible...

Cunhantã* at the prow of a casco*, entering an igapó*.

Above:
The Pico da Neblina (Foggy Peak) at sunset as seen from the southeast side from the Bacia do Gelo. The shadow at the base of the peak is that of the Serra do Ouro. The peak rises to 3,014 meters above sea level and is the highest mountain in Brazil. The peak is rarely seen because of the thick fog that almost invariably covers the it and lends it its name.

Left:
Serra do Padre, as seen from Maturacá — Amazonas.

Right:
Lake near the mouth of the Urubu River, a tributary on the left bank of the Amazon River.

Landscapes

Forest of the upper Negro River; the landscape is unchanging through hours of flying.

The Amazon Plains

It is very common for people to think of the Amazon region as one vast plain wholly covered by an exuberant mantle of forest. This idea has little to do with reality. In fact, the Amazon region shelters savannas, plains, mountains, and even dunes.

We are well aware that in the Amazon landscape, the most dominant figure is the forest itself, dense and seething with life, featuring enormously tall centuries old trees. However, flying over the state of Roraima, for example, we are faced with unexpected landscapes that prompt us to question this image of the Amazon region. The forest suddenly gives way to savannas and the scenery changes completely. Hundreds of lakes sparkle in the midst of extensive grasslands. Far in the background, on the horizon, small isolated hills – known as "islands" – still feature dense vegetation. Recent geological research has showed

On the left:
Landscape on the Negro River near São Gabriel da Cachoeira.

39

Artist and researcher Roland Stevenson, author of the book entitled "Shedding Light on Amazon Mysteries" (*Uma luz sobre os mistérios amazônicos* – Manaus, 1994) which features research on the ethnic diversity of the Amazon region, and covers other important themes such as the Legend of El Dorado.

Excerpt from the book:
"The origin of the Amazon Indians... is still an enigma... where did they come from? What routes and means did they use to arrive here? What mixtures have they undergone? All of these questions are still awaiting clearer and more precise answers. There are also the mythological enigmas of the Amazon, such as the El Dorado, Parime Lake, the white Indians, the Amazons..."

that the "islands" and elevations with dense vegetation were once the actual islands of a large lake, the waters of which drained off into the Branco River due to erosion and tectonic factors.

Plastic artist Roland Stevenson has been carrying out research on the Roraima grasslands and surrounding highlands for fifteen years. He states that this was the site of the Parima River where the legendary city of Manoa – the El Dorado – was said to have appeared.

During a recent expedition, Roland Stevenson and geologist Gert Woeltje discovered that the northern region of Roraima, now an immense plain covered by low vegetation (grassland), is none other than the bed of an extinct lake that once covered an area of 80,000 square kilometers and included a part of Guyana. Two other geologists had already expressed this same belief: Salomão Cruz of the National Department of Mineral Research-DNPM, and Frederico Guimarães Cruz of the Special Secretariat for Environment, Science and

Roraima: Pedra Pintada archeological site.

Technology-SEMACT.

Following his expedition, Gert Woeltje explained that extinction of the lake was a relatively recent occurrence, coinciding with the desperate quests of 16th century explorers. According to this geologist, the water level marks can still be observed *in loco* on most of the hills and mountain ranges that defined the margins on the northern side. The hills within the lake, which at the time would have been islands, con-

Roraima Formation: on a flight from Maturacá to Pico da Neblina.

tinue to be so called by the older natives. Depletion of this huge volume of water was due to a geological phenomenon that featured ongoing elevation of the region, a phenomenon known as "positive epirogenesis". Concomitant to this elevation, a fault occurred (the Mucajai fault), and it was through this fault that the water began to escape, and the waters of the Uraricoera River were captured by the Branco River. The geologist's conclusion is that the faster flow of the river waters and the consequent erosion and silting up of the river beds led in time to total depletion of the lake's water.

According to the legend, the city of Manoa, whose palaces had walls of crystal and roofs of gold, grew up on the banks of Lake Parima... That was all that was needed to arouse the Europeans' undying greed.

Researcher Roland Stevenson tells us that "Juan de Salas", governor of the Caribbean island of Margarita, received accounts of fabulous riches near a large lake from the Aruak Indians. Later, Antônio de Berrio defined the exact coordinates of Lake El

Dorado, but despite numerous expeditions along the Orinoco and Caroni rivers, never reached his goal. However, in 1593, by means of peaceful negotiations, his second in command, Domingo de Vera, verified that the natives of the Pacaraima range (on the Brazil-Venezuela borderline) used all sorts of ornaments made of gold on their ears, nose, arms, chest, and so on...

Continuing our flight to the north, we come to the mountainous region of the Roraima Formation. Here we find the characteristic "tepuios", high plateaus with sharp cliffs, which again form a natural border between the forest that climbs up the slopes, and a new and different savanna that occupies the high part of the plateau.

The Pico da Neblina (Foggy Peak) lies further to the west, 3,014 meters above sea level. It is the highest point in Brazil but is only rarely seen in all its splendor because of the fog. When we did get a chance, it lasted no more than a few minutes. A great mass of fog suddenly began rising from the Venezuelan side. It flowed like a waterfall down

View of the Pico da Neblina as seen from the northeastern side. The Pico da Neblina is on the left in the picture. Right of the Pico da Neblina are the "31 de Março" and "Cardona" Peaks. The Brazil-Venezuela border lies on the first slope to the right of the three peaks.

Carapanaúba tree. Its bark is a powerful remedy for liver ailments.

into the valley, and then rose again very quickly – an enchanting example of the play in movement of masses of air.

We finally reached what seemed to be a large plain and its respectable green mantle.

Now, let's imagine that an irresistible adventurous impulse leads us to jump with a parachute and to land, gently, in the top of a great tree, like we see in movies, and to use a liana to descend to the ground. The temperature already changes and the moistness of the air covers our skin. The dense canopy of leaves of all shapes and sizes blanks out the sunlight, and we are left in a very special shade where the sound of the forest stimulates our hearing and arouses our curiosity. After a short march, we note that our itinerary will never be flat, much less straight: the land drops and rises; obstacles oblige us to detour continuously from our original course. We have no doubt that the forest's sobriquet, "green hell", was invented by people who had faced extensive hikes in the forest. If our imaginary march were real, we would require sound physical conditioning, the ability to make quick decisions, patient resistance, and absolute clearness of mind.

And even so, it would not be sufficient. Those who were not born in the forest, who have never lived there, must realize that to survive in this environment requires knowledge and experience that can only be acquired from the natives. In any case, common sense is enough to show that the services of a reliable guide are essential to safety.

Many unwitting visitors have lost their way in the forest thinking merely of going for a short walk. Others, courageous and equipped with all they could have needed to return safely, underestimated the forest's natural traps.

Raymond Maufrais was a French journalist who traveled to French Guiana, determined to cross the unexplored region of the Tumucumaque. With admirable courage and a dog to keep him company, he faced the forest. All that was later found of him was the diary he had written.

Lianas constitute a type of vegetation whose more plentiful or scarce occurrence or absence determine the definition of the various Amazonian ecosystems. Heliotropism makes for abundant growth of lianas and vines on tracts of land that were once cleared for farming and have since been abandoned.

Amazon forest — looking down from above, the spaces are black...

This is a classic in literature about tropical forests. Maufrais clearly expresses man's situation in the face of impossible Nature:

"I can no longer go on. I hunted again all morning with no result... nothing, nothing. The woods and rivers are dead, incredibly empty. I have the impression of undergoing evolution in an immense desert waiting to crush me. My strength wanes with each passing day. At times I ask myself how I will be able to sustain myself.

...Ah! How I feel overcome today; am I going to die here of hunger?

Again, desperation drives me to hunt, delving

into the woods, overturning old tree trunks, searching in hollow trunks, exploring dens, leaves, looking for a turtle, a snake, a lizard – anything that crawls, as I crawl, getting into everything, naked, entangled in spider webs. Obviously, when one seeks a snake to eat, it is impossible to find one. It will be lying in wait where one least expects to discover it, and exactly when one would most like to avoid it. No sign whatsoever of any snake. And the turtles... the turtles that always appear providentially on days of hunger. I explore each and every meter of terrain..."

(MAUFRAIS, Raymond – *Aventuras na Guyana* - 1950)

...looking up from below, the spaces are filled with light.

On the right:

Brassavola martiana – An orchid photographed in the Anavilhanas archipelago. This species is found in the flood plains and *igapós**, and less frequently in vegetation on solid ground. Its pollinator has not yet been discovered, but its attraction strategy includes the exhalation of a strong odor during the night, greenish-white coloring, and a tubular nectar deposit at the base of the flowers beside the ovary. These features indicate that moths (*Lepidoptera, Sphingidae*) may be responsible for pollination as has been mentioned in literature on other species of the same genus.

Seeking light. Shoot of an unidentified tree.

"The river controls life"

Leandro Tocantins

Fern.

As its name implies, the water of the Negro River, throughout its extension of 3,200 km, is completely black. White sand beaches appear during the dry season, making a beautiful contrast to the green of the forest. The rivers on the left bank of the Amazon flow down from the Andes over the rock beds and from the forest the water collects organic material in decomposition that makes the water black and acid.

Although nearly all the rivers on the right bank come from the Andes, they are much longer than those of the left bank. The rivers on the right wind their way through the sandy plains, eroding banks, creating small islands only to destroy them almost immediately, dragging away villages and trees, precisely because they do not have their own beds. Not even the great Amazon River has its own bed. It moves 800 million tons of sediment each year, and this sediment, thrown into the ocean, is bringing about the growth of the coast of French Guiana and the State of Amapá, as confirmed by satellite images. All the tributaries on the right bank of the Amazon carry tons of earth, minerals, organic material, and other diverse sediment in suspension. The waters of these tributaries are light brown in color and are known as white water rivers.

On the left:
Roraima – Uraricoera River on
the Yanomami Reservation.

*Ribeirinhos** crossing the river at sunset.

Regional boat. Reflection of sunlight on the Negro River.

If on one hand the black rivers are acid, are poor in oxygen, and have less animal life, they make up for these failings by carrying substances that make them healthy and exempt from the proliferation of mosquitoes. The white water rivers are not wholly healthy. They feed life of many species and are perfect breeders of mosquitoes and fish. Their waters are not potable, but due to constant use, the *ribeirinhos** have acquired immunity and use the water they collect from areas of strong currents freely and without any problems.

Left bank of the Solimões River near the Meeting of the Waters.

Approximately 1,100 tributaries empty their waters into the Amazon River, and we arrive at this number counting only the large rivers. Of all the rivers in the whole of the Amazon Basin, only the Amazon River itself empties into the ocean.

The Amazon River is a fertile continent – 7,200 km in length and with average width ranging from 2 to 30 km. Its *várzeas** are extremely rich, and the river harbors a great variety of fish. Literature on the Amazon already features descriptions of 1,500 species of fish, and it is estimated thousands of species are still unknown.

There is good reason for the concentration of villages, towns and cities, along the banks of these muddy rivers, not to mention the *ribeirinhos** who dwell on their banks. Although these riverbank dwellers may go quite some distance to get crystal clear water from the *igarapés** (water that comes from the forest), they insist on living on the riverbanks where food is more abundant.

In the Amazon, with all the nuances this phrase may imply, "the river controls life", to quote Leandro Tocantins.

*Caboclo** home during the flood season. Note that the water has already completely covered the stilts (*palafita**).

When the yearly floods come, the margins of the rivers widen to as much as nearly 100 km. The water rises steadily, usually from three to five centimeters per day, and the difference between the water line at the height of the flood season and the lowest level of the dry season can come to as much as twenty meters. This phenomenon forces *ribeirinhos** to move their cattle to solid ground, out of harm's way. When the flood season is past, they return

*Ribeirinho** squatting on the river bank. This position is of Indian origin and is very common among Amazonian *caboclos**.

Flood

*The water came early
and the great river
spread over the **várzeas**
covering the crops*

*The cabin itself becomes an
island in the river-bank scenery
where threatened **caboclos**
light up the silence with **porongas**
protecting their children
weaving dreams*

Poem by Celdo Braga,
*caboclo** poet and musician.

Even with the water already touching the floor of the *palafitas**, the *ribeirinhos** stay in their homes, and when the waters continue to rise, they either raise the existing floor, or build a new floor above the water line.

to the riverbank land that they know to be more fertile and productive.

"*Caboclos** with their myths and legends, their traditions and extraordinarily rich folklore, their innate religiosity are not only brave, they are lovers of the nature that surrounds them and with which they are so involved that they cannot stand living in cities. When they refer to their native land they do not say they were born in such-and-such a city, but on such-and-such a river: 'I'm from Juruá!' (the Juruá River, tributary on the right bank of the Amazon River)."
(LEANDRO TOCANTINS - excerpt from the book *O Rio Comanda a Vida*).

Flower of a bush in
the undergrowth
(*Rubiaceae*).

Plant and Animal Life

Water lily (*Nymphaea* sp.).
An aquatic plant very
common in still waters.

The Wise Gardener

Walking through the forest, we will find plants and flowers that are familiar to us, common to our own gardens: bromeliads, ficus, orchids, ferns, and so on. It is quite possible that people's need to cultivate greenery in their gardens stems from ancestral roots, from the time when the whole world was green. Who knows, maybe that plant in a vase that we cultivate so tenderly to have some small part of the plant kingdom near us, may be part of that lost world, the memory of which blossoms in our mind... Perhaps it's part of man's efforts to re-establish communication which, in ages long gone, was complete, when plants "spoke" to man and man knew how to "hear" what they said...

On the left:
Orchid (*Scuticaria steelii*).
This species clearly illustrates the feature that gave origin to the name of the genus. Its long cylindrical, hanging leaves look like whips.

Often, when we identify a domesticated plant in the forest and recognize its origin, we feel a sort of familiarity and intimacy at having pinpointed this species as something that is within our realm of knowledge. A more in-depth knowledge of plants and their uses stems from ancient times, more than 12,000 years ago, from an event known as the Neolithic Revolution. The cultivation of previously wild plants was one of the most fantastic episodes of the history of mankind, and since the beginning fulfilled a very important task. It represented not only the formation of large populational centers that gave rise to cities, but also the assurance of survival for those constantly growing populations. Plants represent the base of the food chain for all animals; the origin and guarantee of the existence of our own form of life and of others life forms.

Climbing plants.

Although humanity has not always maintained good relations with the natural world, man has made an effort to keep decorative plants near him. Contemplation of these plants may lead him, consciously or not, back to some moment in our history when we co-existed more harmoniously with the wild, and to encourage feelings of a return to "paradise lost".

Yellow *Ipê* (*Tabebuia* sp.). When in bloom, this tree highlights the forest with the vivid yellow color of its flowers. It is also known as the "bow tree" (*pau-d'arco*) because inhabitants of the region traditionally use its wood to make bows.

In the forest we have the impression that that ancestral link is vigorously reviving. The forest arouses stimuli we have never felt before or brings to mind memories of a past when nature was not merely a refuge from urban life, but the dwelling place of man and of the gods themselves.

However, in order to perceive this wonder, those who travel to the forest must forego for some time the cultural structures of a

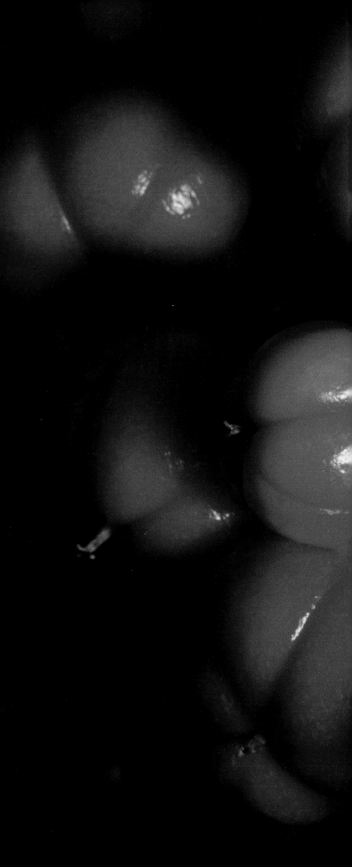

Fruit of the *guaraná** plant (*Paullinia cupana* var. *sorbilis*). The Saterê-Maué Indians who inhabit the region between the Andirá and Maués Rivers have a lovely legend to explain the existence of the *guaraná**. There were once three orphaned children — a beautiful girl and two boys. The boys were lazy and depended on their sister for everything. Due to an undesired pregnancy, the girl gave birth to a boy with beautiful black eyes. The boy's uncles, jealous and full of envy, killed the boy when he was five years old. The mother, seeing her child dead, removed the beautiful eyes before her brothers cremated the body, and planted them as seeds, begging Tupã, the Indians' supreme divinity, to return them to life in the form of a plant. This was the origin of *guaraná**, a plant with extraordinary medicinal powers, tonic and aphrodisiac.

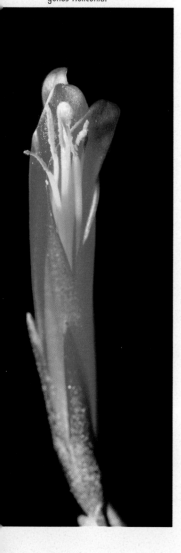

One variety of the genus *Heliconia*.

civilization that never ceases to change nature, and with which, unfortunately, it has established a hostile relationship. Only when we manage to surpass the limits of our daily routine and of the artificial structures that surround us is our soul capable of opening up to perception, and our conscience stops judging and assumes the role of apprentice to a an unending world of knowledge.

We begin to distinguish shapes in what had previously seemed to be a uniformly green and monotonous world. Our wanderings through the forest turn into a voyage rich in happenings: there is a steady procession of novelties. For a few instants, we feel that we have already established a mental integration with nature itself, as we can imagine having happened with our ancestors.

The beings of nature live in a dimension that our senses cannot perceive, but if we train our sensitivity we will be capable of glimpsing them by using the extraordinary powers of our fantasy.

It was not by chance that peoples of different cultures, isolated from one another, came to similar conclusions in regard to the observation of nature, and therein built their sanctuaries to adore their gods – this when nature itself was not the highest expression of all that was held sacred. It is known that imagination limitlessly stimulates the potential for knowledge, imagination itself being a form of knowledge. With a fertile imagination, we can make fantastic trips through the greatest Garden on Earth, where the wisest of all Gardeners provides all sorts of wonders.

Cattleya violacea. Orchid photographed in the Anavilhanas archipelago. The most popular of Amazonian orchids, it is also among those most commonly removed from their natural habitat by "orchid lovers" who, due to lack of information on how to grow them, allow the plants to die. Despite wide distribution, proliferation is sparse, and the plant is already extinct in various regions.

On the right:
A pollinating bat visiting the
flowers of the *sumaumeira**
(*Ceiba pentandra*).
This photo was snapped at
night, when visitors to the
flower feast on the abundant
and delicious nectar at the top
of the *sumaumeira**. The
visitors get covered with
pollen and carry it from one
flower to another, thus
fulfilling their role in
fecundation, and repaying
their host's generosity.

This Garden, devoid of fences or borders, contains the fertile seeds of all gardens, and increasingly arouses our admiration and our imagination. When we return to civilization, we return armed with humility and sensitivity, and immunized against the destructive materialism that has invaded the world. One day we will discover the true reason for our inborn desire to live with plants: we will regain the plant kingdom that lies dormant in each and every one of us.

One variety of the
genus *Heliconia*.

The Kingdom of Biodiversity

Tropical forests shelter a dynamic world, living and full of all sorts of life forms, from the genes that inhabit the low brush, seeking sunlight, to an insect or a tapir, the largest mammal of the Amazon jungle. The biodiversity of the forest is immeasurable. One sole small insect among the hundreds of thousands of existing species may contain the genes necessary to

Brassia lanceana.
Orchid photographed in
the Mariuá archipelago,
at the mouth of the
Branco River.

renew animal cells. Likewise, the leaves of some certain tree may contain the genes which, if duly studied, could enrich the collection of plants that may help cure illness – cures that man has been unable to find in laboratories.

Plants commonly used for food are undergoing the degenerative effects of insecticides and are in need of enrichment. The plants of tropical forests have been living for millions of years, resisting storms and the attack of natural enemies, overcoming the adversities of nature. Transferring this degree of resistance to food plants would definitely benefit mankind.

That's the reason for wanting to preserve the native forest, because that is where we may find

Cigana or Hoatzin
(*Opisthocomus hoatzin*).

Flock of Hoatzins
(*Opisthocomus hoatzin*).
These birds usually live
on the shores of rivers
and *igapós**. They feed
exclusively on vegetal
material and their flying
is limited to short
clumsy flights from one
tree to another.

Shadow of a tarantula.

On the right:
Moth – unidentified.
Note the impression of a
face on its back.

Spider – unidentified.

Red howler monkey (*Aloutta seniculus*).
The howler monkeys live in troops led by the
oldest male who is called the "*capelão*"
(chaplain). In the morning and evening,
especially when the weather is about to
change, they howl (or, as the natives say,
"snort"), in unison, at the top of a tall tree.
On such occasions, their voices can be heard
from a great distance.
The "chaplain", in his patriarchal role, is
responsible for guarding against imminent
danger, such as in cases when the troop is
raiding a plantation. He sounds the alarm from
his observation post, and the natives say that
he is punished when he fails to give timely
warning of an enemy's approach.

The "parauacu-branco"
(*Pithecia albicans*)
measures 30 to 40 cm in
body length, plus about
the same length of tail.
Both body and tail are
covered with long thick fur.

The red-faced or bald Uakari (*Cacajao calvus*). This monkey is also known as "English monkey" in some places because of its red face.

the genes that cure illnesses or make man healthier. To live with the mystery of nature and at the same time demand development and well being for forest dwellers is a major dilemma, and one that stirs up interest in our current civilization.

Among other mysteries, the Amazon forest has its own music. Gastão Cruls expressed it as follows:

"Suddenly, wounding the silence of the bush, we heard a scale of clear, passionate, musical

Humboldt's wooly monkey (*Lagothrix lagothricha*) changing trees.
Tamed by *caboclos**, these monkeys become serious and mild-mannered. Their behavior in the forest is quite the contrary – impudent and challenging.

A baby Humboldt's wooly monkey (*Lagothrix lagothricha*).

sounds. And then a succession of other ranges, higher and lower tones, but all in crystal clear timbres that vibrated in the air for quite some time. Finally, in the sweetest harmony, a ruffle of twittering and trills, here embroidered with pizzicatos, there interspersed with long tremolos and improvised variations, lingering on quarrelsome notes and dying harmonies, or then rising up to lively registers and happy trilling. And there was a bit of everything in that music: silvery vocalizations, violin and zither notes, arpeggios, the strident notes of the sistrum and the softness of the flute, the jingling of many bells...

But who could this magic vocalist or incomparable instrumentalist be?

Perhaps some saucy *saci* (a mythical Brazilian mischief maker) or a winged forest genie... And my eyes, accompanying the others, wandered through the immense canopy of green fronds from whence the caressing and enfolding melody seemed to come. Suddenly silence reigned again, an unforeseen and nearly supernatural silence in which not the slightest whisper of a wing was to be heard...

But who is it?

It's the organ wren (*uirapuru*), an unattractive little bird, but one that has a throat of pure gold. It is very difficult to see the uirapuru because it likes to sing in the highest branches. However, sometimes we can discover where it is because all the other birds come from far and wide to hear it sing, landing near its hiding place".

(GASTÃO CRULS – *Amazônia Misteriosa* - 1953)

The "Amazonian Aerial Plant Project" sponsored by the Amazonas State Government documents epiphytic vegetation and life in the tree-tops. The picture shows Claudio Principe, one of the project's tree-climbers, attracting a wooly monkey.

Humboldt's wooly monkey.

Black-capped capuchin (*Cebus a. apella*). These monkeys live in large troops and are quite daring. They easily become accustomed to humans, but are not often kept as pets because they're too curious and full of mischief. For example: the photo on the right gives the impression that the monkey is dreamily contemplating the wild passionflower. That was not the case at all. He was pestering the photographer who had initially focused the flower itself when the monkey suddenly appeared, grabbed the flower, and gobbled it up. Had he known that the photographer was quite pleased with his antics he probably would not have shown up at all. It's a good example of typical capuchin behavior.

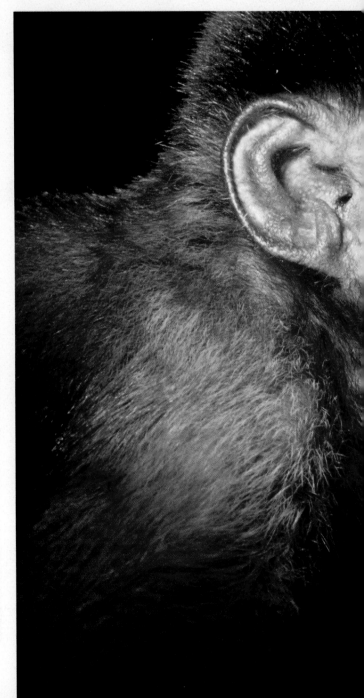

The black spider-monkey (*Ateles paniscus*) features disproportionately long extremities. Its tail is much longer than its body. Spider monkeys are easily tamed by the *caboclos**. Although they have very wrinkled faces that make them look old, they are very fun-loving and comical, a character that matches their ungainly bodies.

"Mangangá" (*Xylocopa* sp.), a type of wasp, on an annatto flower - *urucu** (*Bixa orellana*),

Moth – unidentified.

Moth of the *Arctidae* family.

The Amazon has the largest tropical forest of the planet, covering nearly 60% of Brazil's territory. It represents two-thirds of the earth's tropical forest, about 3.5 million square kilometers of Brazilian area. Only the area of the State of Amazonas is sufficient to hold the entire European continent! Readers will note that there is the State of Amazonas (a unit of the Brazilian federation), the Brazilian Amazon Region (the area of Amazon forest that includes the states of Amazonas, Pará, Amapá, Rondônia, Roraima, Acre, Tocantins, and part of Maranhão), and there is still the International Amazon Region which includes the South

American countries that have Amazon forest within their territory.

Insects of a vast collection are classified and conserved in a large room at the INPA* Entomology Department. There one can get some idea of the surprising complexity and diversity of the Amazon ecosystems. There are thirty million species of insects in the world – one third of them are in the Amazon. Ulysses Barbosa, a technician who takes care of the INPA* collection, jokingly says that there are enough insects to build a whole tree using the countless species of stick-insects (*bichos-páu**) and leaf-insects (*bichos-folha**) that can be light green like new leaves, spotted like old leaves, or even the color of dry leaves. Our imaginary tree is thus ready. Eyes with little training in distinguishing forest beings could well pass right by this "insect" tree without even suspecting it wasn't real.

The Amazonian biodiversity is fantastic. Researchers have already identified the genus and species of about 30,000 plants, but they estimate that there are from five to thirty million

Caterpillars - unidentified.

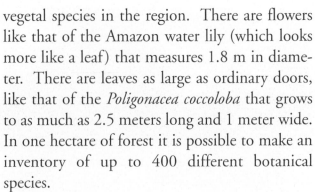

vegetal species in the region. There are flowers like that of the Amazon water lily (which looks more like a leaf) that measures 1.8 m in diameter. There are leaves as large as ordinary doors, like that of the *Poligonacea coccoloba* that grows to as much as 2.5 meters long and 1 meter wide. In one hectare of forest it is possible to make an inventory of up to 400 different botanical species.

Gonzalo Fernandez de Oviedo y Valdés, in *Crônica da História do Mundo Novo*, says:

Fungus photographed in the forest undergrowth. Fungi and bacteria that proliferate in the undergrowth play an essential role in the Amazon forest ecosystems; decomposing organic material, such as the trunks of fallen trees, and leaves that cover the earth, is integrated into the soil much more quickly due to the action of fungi in the form of nutrients (nitrogen), which explains such luxuriant forest growth in poor soil.

"The trees of these Indies are incredibly numerous and many parts of the land are covered with them; there are such great differences among them, their dimensions, their trunks, branches and bark and... the fruits and flowers, that not even the Indians know them... At times, those who find themselves in these woods cannot even see the sky (because the trees are so high, dense, and richly branched)...".

The first explorers never tired of expressing their awe for the grandiose spectacle that nature offered them on their trips to the Amazon.

"If travelers see a certain species and want to find another sample, they will look all over for it. They may look for a long time, see trees of various shapes, sizes, and colors, but rarely will they find two the same. Generally, they are induced by some similarity to look more closely at some species, but upon close inspection, they will find

Roots of a palm tree. Although the roots are aerial at this stage, they will continue to grow until they reach the earth.

Grasshoppers mating.

that it is different. They may even manage to find the same species, but usually they just have to conform themselves and wait for the opportunity to crop up by chance."

(ALFRED RUSSEL WALLACE, 19th century English botanist, from a report on a Botanical Expedition to the Amazon.)

Philip W. Fearnside, researcher of the INPA* Ecology Department, states that "in the

83

Weevil, palm borer
(*Curculio* sp.).

"Buxixu de formiga" (*Tococa*
sp.), a myrmecophilous plant.

Amazon there is a very close relation between the plant and animal kingdoms. Unlike Asian forests, where the main pollinating and seed dispersing agent is the wind, here pollen is carried by insects, and seeds are mainly dispersed by animals (birds, small rodents, monkeys, and so on). The reason for the lack of concentration of plant species in one same area is the extensive presence of seed predators near the trees. Thus, only those seeds transported some distance by dispersor animals will have a chance to germinate".

Insects present the largest number of existing species. Fearnside continues: "During an experiment carried out in the '70s with a view to making an inventory of insects, a strong dose of insecticide was applied to the tree tops. As of that moment, our estimate of the number of insect species on earth was upgraded from 10 to 30 million, based on the number of different insects collected at the foot of those trees, especially beetles. Thus, theoretically, what determines diversity is generally the diversity of the plant cover: the trees determine the forest's structure, the type of climate, and microclimate. When the trees are of the same species, as is the case with commercial forestation featuring pine trees or eucalyptus, the great reduction in the number of insect species shows that plant biodiversity is the basis of diversity for other forms of life".

Moth – unidentified.

Catarina S. Motta, researcher of the INPA* Entomology Department, provides more details: "There is a very intimate relationship between angiosperms (plants more highly developed because they produce flowers, fruit, and seeds) and the Lepidoptera (butterflies and moths). Plants serve as food for these insects in their larval state. When the pupa attain the adult stage, they are no longer equipped for chewing, only sucking. Thus, the same species that attacked the leaves of trees in their first phase, contribute actively to pollination in the adult phase when they suck nectar".

A *caba** (micro Hymenoptera) or hornets' nest.

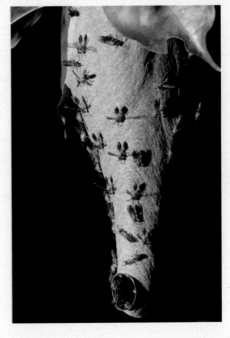

Environmental alterations, the reduction or disappearance of certain species, act on the ecosystems

Butterfly captured
by an ant.

Below, detail of
the same photo.

by changing the original situation, sometimes irreversibly. We can thus imagine the responsibility of human actions on the environment. Civilization is producing an impact of transformations that surpasses ecosystems' capacity for recovery and adaptation. We know that the solution to many of humanity's great problems is to be found in the fabulous files of nature, where we have only begun to discover a few things.

Philip W. Fearnside warns against the danger of superficial delimitation of protected ecological reserves: 112 different ecosystems, defined, among other factors, by the greater concentration of certain insects than others, can be classified only within the Brazilian Amazon region.

Spider – unidentified.

Tarantulas are feared more because of their frightening aspect than their poison. Although their bite is painful, it soon heals.

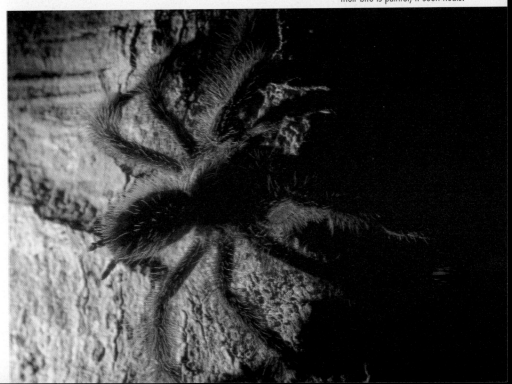

Lizard – unidentified.

Within each of these ecosystems, the organization of life features specific characteristics that we cannot afford to lose. There must be protected areas that comprise all the different types of vegetation. Consequently, the areas must be located based on the 112 ecosystems: open forest, closed forest, forests with few lianas and vines, with an abundance of lianas and vines, and so on.

By practicing subsistence farming, the Indians of the Amazon forest also increase the variety of plants within the range of their

Bicho-folha*.

Black-headed Uakari (*Cacajao melanocephalus*), a monkey
that is outstanding for its exotic "hairdo" and plumed tail.

Wooly monkey (*Lagothrix lagothricha*). This species
uses its tail very skillfully, as though it were a fifth limb.

Note, on page 90, the same phenomenon mentioned on page 27.

dwellings. They select fruits and medicinal forest essences and create true "islands" within the jungle that feature an extraordinary wealth of plant life. Each plant has its use – food, medicine, or magic. When the village is moved to a new site, the population takes along a selection of seeds and plants to be transplanted to the new dwelling place, thus contributing to the conservation and dissemination of species.

The pygmy marmoset (*Cebuella pygmaea*) – the smallest of all Amazonian monkeys – fits in the palm of a hand.

Butterfly on the flower of a "toucan-bill", an exotic plant typical of the Amazon forest.

A tender moment shared by
two wooly monkeys
(*Lagothrix lagothricha*).

Praying mantis (*Mantidae*
family) on a *Cattleya violacea*,
one of the most beautiful
Amazonian orchids.

Brazilian pied tamarin (*Saguinus bicolor*). A small monkey very common in the forests near Manaus.

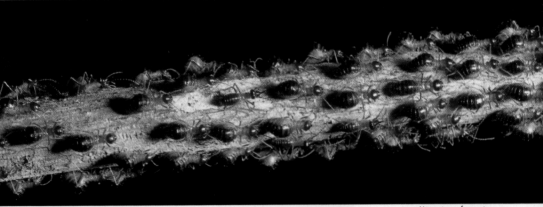

Migration of termites
(*Constrictotermes* sp.).

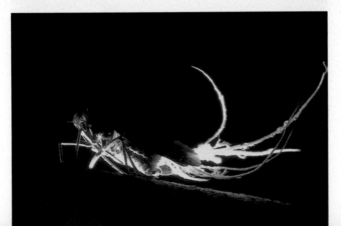

"Rabo-de-galo" (*Fulgoridae*
family); a harmless flying insect
that features "plumes" when it
comes out of its cocoon, whence
its name: "cock's tail".

Head of a *Diptera*
(*Asilidae* Fam.), wild fly.

Chinch bug with offspring on fruit
of the soapberry tree.

Nest of ants — unidentified.

These ants, known as "saúva" or harvester ants (*Ata* sp.), cut leaves and carry them to their nest where they will serve to grow the fungi on which the ants feed.

For example, the Kaiapó Indians recognize and use approximately 600 different plant species classifying fifteen different ecosystems, according to the percentage of tall trees, scrub growth, bushes, or natural plains, as well as considering the presence of water, slopes, and formation of the terrain.

The wisdom of the Indian people was lost together with the Indians themselves who failed to survive contact with "our civilization".

At present, approximately 170,000 "known" Indians live on the Amazon Indian reservations, but we know of at least fifty-three groups of Indians that are still isolated, and have had no contact with "our civilization". These are the last survivors of the native Amazonian ethnic groups.

Evidence shows that the first inhabitants of the Amazon lived 12,000 years ago. However,

Butterfly in the forest.

virtually nothing is known about these ancient Amazon civilizations. There were more than six million Indians in Brazil 500 years ago, mostly in the Amazon region. There are now only 300,000 in the country – a mere 5% of the population descending from the native inhabitants present upon the first contact with the Portuguese colonizers.

"Apuí" (*Clusia* sp.).
Of all the trees in the Amazon forest, the "apuí" is that which most calls attention
due to its unique strategies. The seeds, carried by birds, sprout on the higher
branches, sending out shoots that grow straight down to the ground where they
take root. These shoots then multiply horizontally, literally embracing the host
tree, and replacing it. But not all trees give themselves up to this embrace: no
matter how many "apuí" seeds sprout on the *sumaumeira**, there is no record of
any *sumaumeira** ever having been dominated.

Tree orchid
(*Heterostemon ellipticus*).

On the right:
Beetle (*Diactor bilineatus*).
Commonly found among the
leaves of the wild
passionflower plant.

Praying mantis
(*Mantidae* family).

Jaguar (in Tupi - *ya'wara*)
(*Panthera* [jaguarius] *onca*).
The jaguar climbs trees with the
same ease that it shows in
crossing rivers. No other animal
can equal it in high jumps or
broad jumps, and added to this
ability are its skills as a shrewd
and wily master hunter.
Jaguars prefer to hunt at dusk.
After subduing their prey, they
carry it to a hiding place where
they eat their fill, saving any
leftovers for the next day.
Jaguars betray their presence by
a repetitive dry clicking sound
they make by nervously twitching
their ears, producing a sound
similar to that of muffled
castanets.

Fungi photographed in
the forest undergrowth.

U-iara, the *boto vermelho**

The Amazon rivers are the home of several types of cetaceans: *tucuxi*, gray, black, and red. This last, the *boto vermelho**, is classified as *Inia geoffrensis*. After Jacques Cousteau's expedition to the Amazon, this cetacean was erroneously labeled as "pink". However, as the Inia has always been known as "red", the *boto vermelho**, by *ribeirinhos** as well as by INPA* researchers, this new and misguided denomination aroused comments on the part of some people.

Botos, like all cetaceans, feature a proportionately larger brain than that of man. Intelligent, respected, and even feared, they are attractive not only because of their color, but also because of their skill as swimmers and divers. They irritate those who fish with nets or *malhadeiras** because they damage the nets when they "steal" fish from the catch. On the other hand, during night fish-

INPA* researchers Fernando Rosas and Francisco Collares observe the behavior of the *boto vermelho**, temporarily confined near the shore of the Tapajós River.

Boto vermelho* floating.

ing (*facheação**) with lantern and spear, they are friendly and helpful partners. They scare the fish away from the riverbank and if the spear fisher doesn't hit it, the boto easily catches it.

The fishermen do not harm *botos**. There are countless stories of "bad" fishermen who attacked some boto with disastrous consequences. To people of the Amazon region, to harm a boto is to ask for bad luck and unhappiness.

Salt-water porpoises emit more than sixty distinct sounds and according to researchers these sounds constitute words with which they communicate with one another. The Amazon *botos* are believed to have come from the ocean and adapted perfectly to the environment. This adaptation may have occurred due to the abundance of food.

At the time of the region's cyclical floods, the waters invade the forest and the *botos*, thanks to their flexible bodies, manage to twist and turn among the roots and trunks, feeding heartily on the fish that hide in such places. These mammals have a very sophisticated radar system, with a structure that allows them to emit ultrasound waves (the so-called "melon" or hump) that reflect on solid bodies. The sound waves return as echoes, guiding the *botos* through black or muddy water despite the reduced visibility.

Botos have a great deal of freedom. They are helpful and affectionate to man. They issue characteristic sounds that bring to mind the pleasant laughter of the *caboclo**. Some say that *botos** do their best to save people in danger of drowning, or to defend them from aquatic predators.

Photographer's note: when the *boto vermelho** floated, Chico, the clever Ubim River fisherman who accompanied us on this photo expedition said: "That's him! That's the nation's chief!", and he laughed happily, like a child. "Take a picture of him! He's the chief of the *boto* nation!".

Botos* have a peculiar feature: their genitalia is similar to that of men and women. This is the reason for stories of sexual relations between men and female *botos*, or between women and male *botos*. There are even cases of children registered as "son or daughter of the *boto*".

A woman cannot travel by canoe during her menstrual cycle because the boto will follow her; if she is not careful, she may even be thrown out of the canoe. According to Amazon region belief, when *ribeirinhos** throw parties in their riverbank *barracões**, or on the *beiradão**, the *boto*, impeccably dressed in hat and white clothes, mixes in with

108

Flying over Janauacá Lake, we came upon a *boto vermelho** 'playing', doing its tumbling act in the water. We have no doubt whatsoever in regard to applying the literal meaning of the word 'play', with all the human and emotional connotations the word implies.

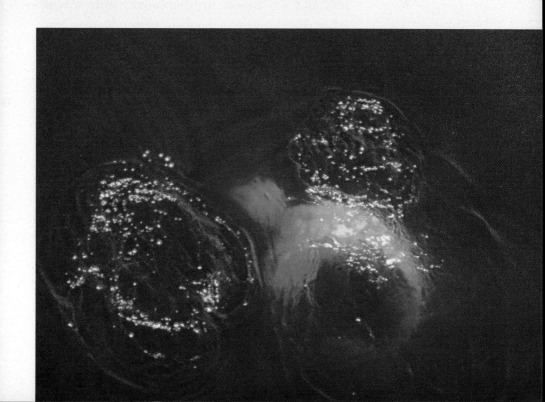

Pink dolphins (*boto**)
are very skillful at
swimming among the
sunken trunks and roots
of the *igapó** in search
of their prey.

the men. He is always elegant, polite, and a skill-ful dancer, and he attracts the attention of women who immediately fall for him. The *boto* chooses a woman with whom he will dance all night long, while the men cast envious and jealous looks at him. The woman chosen is always the most attractive and sought after *cabocla** of the gather-ing, and she almost invariably falls in love with what she thinks is a handsome young man and goes out to walk with him under the cacau or *cupuaçu** trees. Months later this young woman, still enchanted and longing for the caress of the most charming "man" she ever met, shows the first signs of an unplanned preg-nancy... "It was the *boto*!" When she goes to register the child, the single woman proudly states: "the father of the child is the *boto*!"

On any white sand beach of the river, in the straw huts or *barracões** of the *coronéis**, there is always some *caboclo** telling stories about pretty girls who were impregnated by a *boto*. In communities of the interior, it is very common for people to accept this behavior on the part of the *boto* and the girls as perfectly natural.

Chico, the fisherman and great storyteller who accompanied us on our search for the *boto vermelho**, told us that his wife's grandfather had met a witch doctor who visited the city of the *botos* in

INPA* technicians release the *boto vermelho** after collecting data and studying the behavior of this aquatic mammal.

111

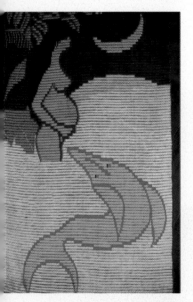

Folk representations of the *boto vermelho** legend.

the depths of the river. The grandfather was curious and asked the witch doctor to take him along on his next visit to the enchanted city. The witch doctor agreed, but on one condition: that he was not to accept anything that was offered to eat or drink, because if he did, he would never return home. When they arrived at the enchanted city, the *botos* were having a great party, singing, eating, drinking and dancing happily. The two visitors were careful not to accept any food or drink, and danced with the *botos* until it was time to return. The grandfather and the witch doctor would have liked to have stayed there forever, but they said farewell to the partying *botos* and returned to the riverbank. The grandfather was amazed to see that his clothes were still dry, despite his having worn them when diving into the river...

The Amazon *caboclos** frequently refer to stories about the enchanted *boto* kingdom in the depths of the waters. If we take into account how people can fantasize or tell stories about their experiences and what exists or can possibly exist, we will be awed by the fact that the *botos* have an enchanted city, with an extraordinary kingdom, much richer than that of humankind.

In a recent congress on esoteric matters held in São Paulo, one of the clairvoyants explained that dolphins come from Sirius, the brightest star in the sky, situated in the Constellation Canis Major. They are very highly developed, with intelligence greater than that of humans, and "decided" to inhabit our planet to "contribute" to man's evolution.

These stories may be unreal, but they do show surprising similarities. People who live in the Amazon or have become integrated with that region's nature no longer doubt these stories about the *boto*. There are hundreds of them, and to judge by the way people speak of them, anything may be possible...

Who can actually claim to know the Amazon and its mysteries?

Sincere researchers of the Amazon's natural resources humbly acknowledge that they know nothing, and that from one day to the next a new fact may appear that will revolutionize what had previously been considered absurd. For those who venture to "discover" the Amazon, a sub-

There is a close mythological relationship between native women and the *boto vermelho**. It is said that when a *boto* passes in the shadow of a *cunhã**, the woman gets pregnant; that a single person who sees a *boto* floating three times will be married in that same year; and that married women must look the other way when a *boto* appears, because if they look on the *boto* three times, they will be widowed in that same year.

stantial capacity for selflessness and sensitivity is essential. They must be able to glimpse the poetry and the "fantastic" when faced with the unknown, and to run the risk of complete lack of definition, even if only for a few moments...

Who knows what about the Amazon?

Could it perhaps be the *boto vermelho**?...

...Could the *boto* be the holder of the secret that enfolds the forest, the waters, and all the beings that comprise this "Great Work"?

Cacilda Barbosa, author of short stories about the Amazon, relates something very interesting in a book featuring regional "tales":

Livia Monami, Italian biologist and journalist who took part in the expedition to the Tapajós River.

The *jaraqui** (*Semaprochilodus brama*) tries to escape from the *boto**, but it will probably not be so lucky on the next dive. Note the profile of the *boto** lying in wait just below the surface. The *jaraqui** is one of this aquatic mammal's favorite meals, as is the *tucunaré**. There is an old saying in the region: "he who tries the *jaraqui** never leaves" - a reference to visitors who fall in love with the region and just stay on.

"The *boto* was performing his pirouettes in the river on a beautiful sunny morning when Iara, "Mother of the Waters", called him over to a clump of *cumaru* (*Dipteryx odorata*) and invited him to a dance that was to be held at the end of the month in the *barracão** of *Coronel** Procópio, the most popular of the surrounding area.

The *boto* asked, 'Iara, how can I dance if I

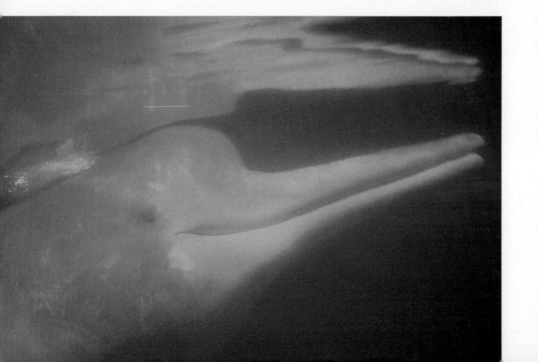

don't have legs?'

Iara answered, 'Let's call the fairy godmother of the forest, Dona Ci. She'll know what to do'.

And so they began to invoke the fairy godmother. She soon appeared saying she was at their disposition, and they told her what they wanted.

The godmother agreed: 'All right, at the next full moon I will be here to help the *boto*, and the two of you will go to the dance'.

When the moon was enormous and majestic, the fairy godmother appeared all dressed in white. She called the boto and said:

'I'm going to transform you into the most elegant man of the party. But on the stroke of 3:00 a.m. you must go straight back to the river.

The *boto* took Iara in his arms, carried her up the riverbank, and set her down near a clump of banana trees. Iara quickly hid her tail under the leaves, while the *boto* went into to the hall all decked out for the party. A *caboclo** approached Iara and started a conversation,

The *boto vermelho** features a protuberance on the head - known as the "mellon" - from which it issues ultrasonic sound waves that work like radar to guide these mammals in waters where visibility is poor.

admiring the beauty of this young woman who refused to dance that night no matter how much he insisted.

When the *boto* entered the hall, the men looked at him with envy because he was the most charming of all the men, and some even went so far as to suggest that they expel him.

He paid them no heed, looked around, chose the prettiest and most skilled of the young women and led her onto the floor to dance followed by admiring glances.

Every now and then he would leave his partner and take some tidbit and a *guaraná** to Iara who remained outside in *Coronel** Procópio's yard entertaining the *caboclo**.

The beautiful *cabocla** the boto had chosen to dance with fell madly in love with him and hung onto him the whole night. However, when the big clock in the hall began to strike three, the

*Curumim** feeding a *jaraqui** to the *boto vermelho**.

120

young man suddenly released his partner, ran out to the yard, picked up Iara, and ran to the river-bank. The girl with whom he had danced all night long was indignant at his escape and ran after him, shouting, begging him to stay on at the dance, all in vain. He and Iara threw themselves into the river, and the girl dove into the river after them. It was only when the three came to the surface that the *boto* noticed that he had been dancing all night with the *Cobra- Grande*... "

Boto vermelho*.
An underwater photograph taken in the Tapajós River.

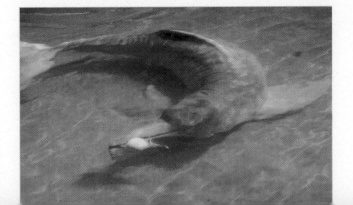

Aerial photo of *botos vermelhos**
in the waters of the Negro River.

Who knows what about the Amazon?
Could it perhaps be the *boto vermelho**?…
…Could the *boto* be the holder of the secret
that enfolds the forest, the waters, and all the
beings that comprise this "Great Work"?

A *boto vermelho**
accompanies a
ferryboat crossing
the Negro River.

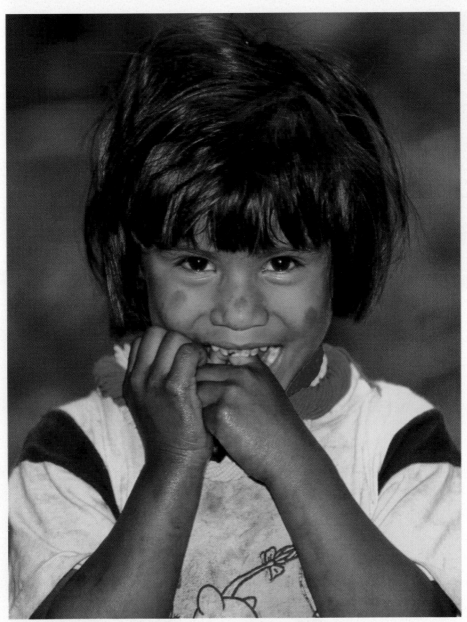

*Curumim** of the Makiritari ethnic group of Indians living in Brazil and Venezuela. They speak the *Yekuana* language, and on the Brazilian side are called *Maiongong*.

Indians and *Caboclos**

Walahari-á

We met Walahari-á on the Yanomami Indian
Reservation on the Serra das Surucucus. Every
time we pronounced the little Indian's name, or
at least what we thought was his name as he had
been identified by indiscreet conversations
among the *curumins**, he and the other children
would laugh at us. In fact, neither he nor any of
the others directly told us their names. Indians
do not say their own names in front of strangers

Walahari-á, a Yanomami
*curumim**, extracts dye from
plants to paint his face.

124

because this lowers their defense and provides access to their soul. When we managed to pronounce the name "Walahari-á" properly a few days later he gave us some very suspicious looks. However, our friendship had already been consolidated, and mutual confidence was quickly restored.

Walahari-á followed researchers on their expedition to Serra das Surucucus showing a keen interest in the collection of insects and other aquatic specimens.

Throughout the time that our team spent in the Surucucu camp, Walahari-á sought out our company and paid attention to everything we did. Our intuitive communication consisting of questions and answers was carried out in the universal language of signs and gestures.

The *curumim** looks at material collected by the researchers.

Aiming (above), climbing trees (on the right), and all other skills related to life in the forest come naturally to the *curumim**.

While the researchers collect aquatic specimens, Walahari-á soon learns to capture flying insects.

One morning we were preparing to explore an Indian trail west of the base. After a three-hour hike down the slopes of the Surucucus we came to the site of an old mission, now abandoned. Although nothing had been combined, Walahari-á accompanied us.

In the forest, the *curumim** acted as though he were playing in his own back yard. He proved himself extremely skillful in handling the machete: he would cut long thin rods for spears that he would throw at the anthills without hiding his satisfaction in feeling our interest in his games. We would stop and pay attention to his gestures, asking him, in nonverbal language, about animals, plants, or fruit that we saw along the way. We learned a lot from him and he learned from us.

When we first met the *curumim** we called him the "boy with the bow" because he always had a bow and arrow in his hands. When he accompanied us he was unarmed. We asked him where he had left his bow and he answered that it had broken, so we asked him to make another right there. We put our heavy backpacks on the ground expecting a lengthy wait. But Walahará, quick and sure, identified a tree, made a slash in it and pulled off some bark to make the *envira**, working it between his hands and legs. In a few minutes he showed us a fine, white, uniform line, very resistant and comparable to a nylon line. Then, looking around like a carpenter in his workshop, he soon found the branch that was to become a flexible and effective bow. After working the wood, he tied the line with a knot that would do justice to an experienced sailor, and reaching under the leaves, pulled out a rod that would make a good arrow, as though it had been right there just waiting for him all along.

We noticed that the little Indian did not cut a green rod that would be too heavy and too flexible.

The bow and arrow were ready within a few minutes. Showing us his weapon, he smiled that generous smile common to children who get what they want. And for the first time, we felt that the situation was inverted. It was no longer the Indian who was awed at the sight of some white man's machine, but white men acknowledging the Indian's skill!

When aiming the arrow, he would point the direction the arrow was to go with the index fin-

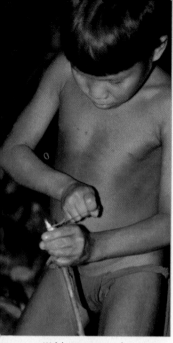

ger of the right hand that held the arrow. He rarely missed his target.

We continued our march to the *igarapé** in the middle of the valley to collect aquatic insects, fish, mollusks, and shrimp. Walahari-á enthusiastically took part in everything. He was a skillful helper, showing interest especially in capturing butterflies and other flying insects. He was in his own element and he knew how to move about very nimbly without scaring off the insects. He would catch them very quickly, and gave us lessons on how to move about in the forest.

Walahari-á cuts a stick, prepares a line made from fiber extracted from the bark of a tree (*envira**), and within a few minutes has built himself a bow.

Assembling the bow.

Inborn aptitude and instructive games will transform the *curumim** into a hunter.

Yanomami village on the Auaris River. Photographer's note: "To me, this image represents one of the most decisive moments of my career in that it defined my way of working and of how to direction my quest for the message to be transmitted. That

embrace summarizes the meaning of human nature. I took part in that moment, unnoticed and without interfering in any way, but capturing and amplifying a moment worthy of reflection in our world so lacking in affection and loving care".

Experiencing Nature

To Walahari-á, those were different days. He
learned something from us, and we learned from
him. He showed us many things and with such

Yanomami *maloca**
in the Serra das
Surucucus region.

determination that we were able to perceive his
potential to become a great leader of his people
thanks to his intelligence, reasoning, skill, dex-
terity, and his capacity to communicate. Given
the Indians' in-depth knowledge of the forest
and experience with nature, white men certainly
have much to learn from them.

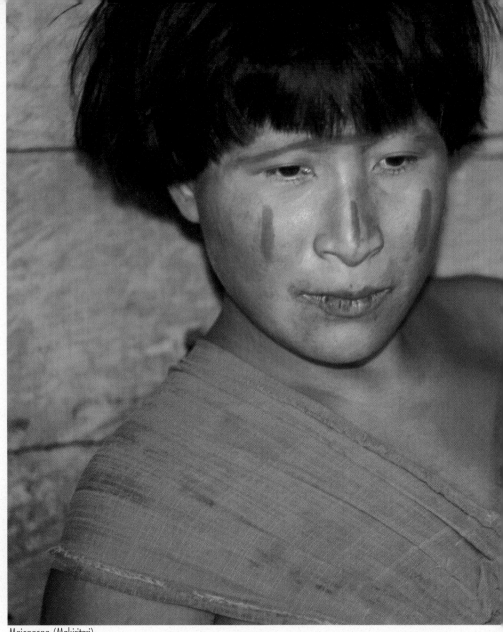

Maiongong (Makiritari)
mother nursing her child.

Our little friend has the wisdom of centuries. It is up to "civilized" people to overcome their tiring and stressful routine, their craving for individual wealth and for the sophisticated lifestyle, to observe the peace, tranquility, and serenity of the life of Indians in the forest. To us it seems inhospitable, aggressive, and mysteri-

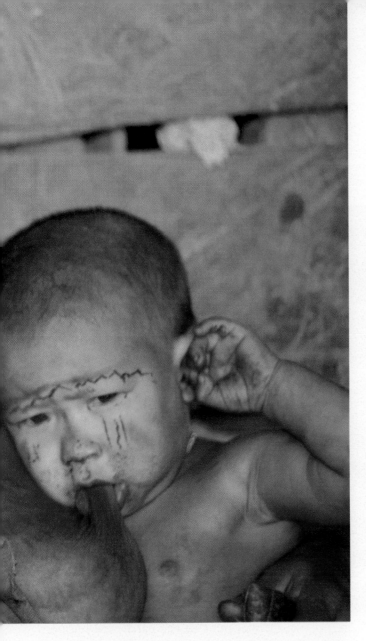

ous, but to the Indians it is familiar, friendly, generous, and fertile.

Therefore, there must be more humility on our part to acknowledge that people of the forest carry within themselves an extraordinary heritage of history and culture to be unveiled and assimilated by modern man. This may be the solution for our culture, contradictorily sophisticated, and yet unable to offer that inner peace that comes from a harmonious relationship with the environment.

Yanomami Indian making a paddle.

On the right:
Yanomami Indian woman of the Surucucus village. The green tobacco leaves, besides serving as ornamentation, are carried on the body to dry.

" ... I saw thousands of buffalo rotting on the plains, abandoned there by the white men who shot them from the windows of a train in passing. I am a savage and do not understand how the 'iron horse' can be more important than the buffalo that we only kill in order to survive. What will become of the white men without animals? If all the animals disappear, man will die of a great solitude of the spirit. Because everything that happens to the animals will also happen to man, but it is man who belongs to the earth. Man did not weave the net of life: man is merely a part of it. All that man does to the net, he will be doing to himself. What happens to the earth will happen to the sons of the earth. All things are related like the blood that binds one family..."

(Chief Seattle in answer to a letter from the president of the United States proposing to purchase land from the Indians.)

These words, written more than a century ago, show that they are still valid in today's

world and reveal the age-old culture of all the Indians of the American continent. Chief Seattle's message was not heard, and to this day there are fools shooting down buffalo from inside their little trains...

"My people have lived on this earth for a long time, since the time when the world did not yet have the shape it has today. The forest people retain the memory of the creation of the world, of the fundamental principles of life. We feel that we must prevent civilization from offending nature. We all recall days when the world took care of all the people – feeding, caring, lulling us to sleep with the sounds of birdsong, rivers, waterfalls, and forests. Each season taught us

Maiongong (Makiritari) girl carrying firewood.

Yanomami warrior
painted for the hunt.

that there is a right time for each activity. We want to show city dwellers that it is possible for the human race to attain its adventure with nature still living. We want to build a beautiful forest in the hearts of city dwellers; a forest made of friendship, music, and parties. Then we will be able to pacify their spirits so that they can live with the forest people.

This is our message."

(Testimonial of Aílton Krenak, president of the Alliance of the Forest People for the book entitled "Save the Earth").

Previous page: Yanomami mother preparing *beiju**.

Aílton Krenak tells that the house that serves as headquarters of the Embassy of the Union of Indian Nations is located is a building of colonial construction made in the 18th century.

"Historians and architects dance around it... because they have seen a very old house. I just look at them and think: how young these people are... They believe that this construction made in another age is sufficiently antique to inspire their architecture and guide their culture. Do they by any chance know that a Brazil nut tree lives 600 years? That mahogany, jacaranda, or *jequitibá* trees can live as long as 1,200 years? And that they can hear stories of that time sitting under the tree? ... This culture that people call 'western'... all this apparent antiquity is for kindergartners. And they apply this 'antiquity' to the rest of the country. They lack respect for illustrious figures such as this 135-year-old ancient who was once a slave. They lack respect for people like our grandparents who are in the forest and villages as their forebears were for many centuries, teaching their children to tread carefully on the earth".

"My friend Davi Ianomâmi went with me to Athens when I received the award from the Onassis Foundation. There they took us to see beautiful places,

Maiongong (Makiritari) child.

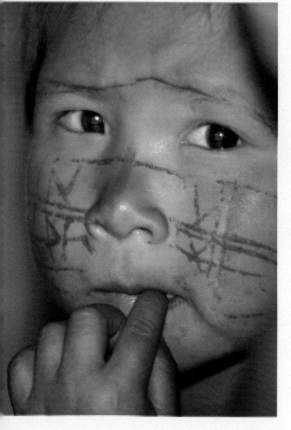

Yanomami Indian
woman in Waikas,
on the Uraricoera
River, peeling
manioc root that
she will use to
make manioc meal.

from the Greek Parliament to the Parthenon.
Some Greek diplomats were very happy to show
their monuments to people of another culture.
One of them said: 'this is 4,000 years old; people come from all over the world to see it.
What's your impression?' Davi answered:
'Now I know where the *garimpeiros** came
from'. This was because the *garimpeiros** were
on his land, destroying forests to build monuments such as those. The look of some of our
village children holds more antiquity than that
monument. Sometimes a medicine man taking
a newborn child in his arms will sing and dance
for the happiness of having seen those eyes.

Yanomami Indian boys.

Later he gives the child the name of an ancestor who passed by here 4,000 years ago and returned in the look of that child to teach ancient chants, rites, and ceremonies. The look of that boy is like the water of the river that passes by every day. It is not the same, but it always brings to mind the same memory. Our oldest monument is not a building or a pyramid. It is our memory."

(Excerpts from an interview granted by Aírton Krenak to Pedro Camargo and Alexandre Mansur – *ANO ZERO* Magazine – February 1992).

Caboclo exracting milk
from the amapa*
(Brosimum parinarioides).*

People of the Backlands

"The population of the Amazon territory that
is cut by countless rivers, *paranás**, *furos**, and
tropical lakes, is almost wholly made up of fish-

ermen and small-plot farmers who practice subsistence farming and fishing, and make handi-
crafts, nearly all consisting of hunting and fishing objects, and tools such as bows, arrows,
spears, the *malhadeira**, nets, fences, ladders and
other implements. The man of the backlands is
always, and at the same time, fisherman, farmer,
artisan, hunter, *juteiro**, lumberjack, nut picker,

*Ribeirinho** in the reflected sunlight.

*seringueiro**, *balateiro**, story teller, medicine man, and many other things."
(ANDRADE, Moacir. *Folclore do Peixe do Amazonas*).

The *caboclo** is like an intermediary stage between two worlds: that of the forest people, and that of the people of technology. No one better than the *caboclo** to take on the defense of the Amazon ecosystems, because he knows this environment and lives in it.

However, the *caboclos** live totally abandoned with only themselves to depend on. Need obliges them to prey on the environment, not so much because they want to, but because they are subject to all sorts of limitations. They lack technical, medical, and educational support – all the basic means of survival and a minimal quality of life.

Manaus – "Baixa da Égua", port of arrival for boats coming from the interior.

Caboclo* boy holding a bunch of *açaí** fruit. *Açaí** wine, a heavy and nutritious beverage rich in iron, is made from the pulp of the fruit.

*Ribeirinhos**

The great majority of the *ribeirinhos** live in houses built on stilts (*palafitas**) because of the great cyclical *enchentes**. They eke out a living from their small *roçados** of manioc, corn, watermelon, winter squash, banana, and near to the houses, fruit trees such as *cupuaçu**, cacau, cof-

Caboclo* children with baby capivaras*.

fee, lemon, oranges, *pupunha**, *tucumã**, mangoes, and others. From the *várzea** and from solid ground they harvest *pequiá, uxi-coroa*, castanha-do-pará*, bacaba*, açaí*, patauá** – an enormous assortment of wild fruits whose seasonal cycles occur regularly – besides medicinal oils, tree bark, roots, and seeds.

They hunt increasingly fewer forest animals.

On the *várzea** perhaps an occasional *capivara** or *paca** that comes to drink water when it fails to rain in the forest, and few others.

The river with its *igapós**, lakes, and *paranás** is their main source of protein.

In their *casco**, they penetrate the aquatic vegetation – *canarana**, *arroz-de-marreca**, *muri**, interspersed by a great variety of water lilies – extremely rich in subaquatic life, or in the *igapós**. They choose the fish according to the time of year, savoring them fresh and tasty at every meal.

Fishing methods vary according to the stage of the *vazante** or *enchente*, and the good fishermen adjust to situations with a versatility that only experience can provide.

The fish families characteristic of lakes and *igapós**, such as the *tucunaré**, *jacundá**, *aruanã**, *traíra**, *jeju** and many others, spawn and care for their fry in the *igapós**.

The *pirarucu**, a much larger fish and very cautious, makes its nest in the coves of lakes or *cabeceiras**, and even in *igapó** areas, as long as there is open sky. The couple takes turns at guarding the nest and when the eggs hatch they care for and protect the fry until they grow to a length of twenty centimeters or more.

In the meantime, the fish heading upstream during the *piracema** form enormous schools on

Line fishing for *pirarucu** (*Arapaima gigas*).

their way to the rivers' headwaters to spawn – *pirapitingas**, *pacus**, *curimatás**, *sardinhas**, *matrinxãs**, *branquinhas**, *jaraquis**, *cubius**, *araris**, *charutos** and countless others.

The presence of the schools is easily detected because of the happy gamboling of the *botos** when faced with such abundance.

The deeper waters shelter the Pimelodidae or catfish family: *piraíbas**, *jaús**, *pirararas**, *surubins**, *piramutabas** and many more.

Fortunately, use of the *timbó**, a poisonous liana which, when macerated, drugs and kills fish indiscriminately, is virtually extinct. The use of *timbó** was a heritage of Indian culture, but the Indians used it very sparingly and only in special situations.

As readers will note, the *ribeirinhos**, true Amazonians, live in a universe of immeasurable wealth that we must protect and preserve.

On the left:
Ribeirinho* preparing a pirarucu* for drying.

Floodlands during the flood season.

From March to September, the Amazon is transformed into a world of waters. The canoes normally used for fishing and for transportation can be tied to the roofs of the *palafitas**. As the water rises, averaging about 3 to 5 centimeters each day, if necessary the *ribeirinhos** raise the floor. They prepare for the high water. The cattle is transferred to solid ground, the floor of the house is raised, and a new lifestyle is improvised. For the smaller farm animals (pigs, chickens, sheep, etc.), and to preserve the small vegetable garden of green onions and parsley, a *maromba** is built next to the house.

Caboclo* making his canoe.

"I doubt there are any conservation laws such as these in the legislation of civilized man: anyone who cuts down or breaks a tree without need, only for fun or mischief, is punished by the Mother of the Forest. Anyone who cuts a *seringueira** in fun or mischief will be punished by the Mother of the *Seringueira**. The Mother of the Water will punish anyone who catches small fish only for fun, kills them, and throws them back into the water. The Mother of the Forest will punish anyone who throws *timbó** into an *igapó** just out of mis-

Moments in the capture of the *pirarucu**.

chief... The river spirits will punish anyone who shoots an arrow into a *boto** just for fun... Women must not board a fisherman's canoe from the prow, but in the middle, or between the middle and the stern. If a woman boards the canoe wrongly, the fisherman will become *pane-ma**... Fishermen, if they are to be lucky on all their fishing trips, must bathe using a new *cuia** and the water of the river they are fishing in.

*Caboclo** proudly exhibits *pirarucu**, the result of his line fishing.

Boat typical of the *ribeirinhos**, near São Gabriel da Cachoeira.

Land flooded during the flood season. Note that the water has already covered the stilts (*palafitas**).

This will make them *marupiara**. The *cuia**
must be unused... Prior to throwing a line to
catch large fish, fishermen must coat the whole
line with tobacco for the fish to get drunk and
not resist being pulled into the canoe... If fishermen see a group of *botos** jumping with their
heads pointing to the headwaters, a big flood is

159

coming. To prevent *panemice**, no fisherman must ever leave his fishing nets or any other implements near *curumins**, because if a *coirão** urinates on the net or on any other fishing gear, not only will the fisherman become *panema**, but none of his gear will ever catch another fish... Anyone who fishes for the *peixe-boi** must be careful not to kill the first one they spot, or more than one on any fishing trip. If they do, they will have bad luck for the rest of their life, and *panema** for any and all fishing trips."
(ANDRADE, Moacir. *Folclore do Peixe do Amazonas*).

Caboclo* opening a Brazil nut seed pod.

Seringueiros*

The precious latex of the *seringueira** flows more freely in the very early hours of the morning. That's when the forest man goes out with his *poronga** on his head and begins his daily task: to cover many kilometers through the lanes of the rubber plantation. Actually, the rubber tappers cover these lanes twice a day. The first time, with a special knife, they bleeds the bark of the tree and place the "mug", a small tin recipient that is attached to the *seringueira** to collect the sap. The second time, around ten o'clock in the morning after a short rest for *rango**, they return along the same lane, collecting the full mugs to take the product to their straw huts. There they smoke the latex. This is known as *defumação**, the first and most primitive phase of rubber processing.

Trunk of a *seringueira**
(*Hevea brasiliensis*)
showing the slashes
made for tapping.

In the beginning of this century, with development of the auto industry, men of the Brazilian northeast were literally thrown into the Amazon forest, an environment they were not very familiar with. "Soldier of rubber" was the nickname these people were dubbed with to make them feel like heroes of a cruel war in a time of peace. They knew nothing of the climate, nature, waters, animals, illnesses, and mosquitoes. Coming from arid land, they worked their way insanely into the damp forest

subjected to the heavy rains, endemic diseases, aggression from Indians, and worst of all, the infamous exploitation on the part of the *seringalista**. The *barracão** system depleted, humiliated, and held thousands of northeasterners as prisoners to be exploited. And this in cases when they didn't shorten the life of these people through hunger, mistreatment, and intensification of diseases typical of the region.

The rubber tappers received no money; everything was taken care of in the *barracão** of the *seringalista**, who sold food to the *seringueiros**. As the workers received minimum wages, they were always in debt to the company store.

In some areas, especially in Rondônia, Acre, the north of Mato Grosso and the south of Pará, the lumberjacks invaded the forest. The agribusinesses owned by multinationals or by *grileiros** from the southern part of the country began to fell trees indiscriminately, clearing the land to make way for enormous extensions of grazing land. Grasses took the place of the *castanheiras** and *seringueiras**, trees that the law stated could not be cut down. Centuries old trees were also felled and medicinal plants, rare plants, many still unknown to botanists, were eradicated.

The *seringueiros** were expelled from their *colocações** or killed. Many put up resistance, among them Chico Mendes, who was capable of rising up against

oppression. He led the forest people, intuitively guided by an unequalled ecological awareness and by a deep-rooted determination to achieve integration with nature.

The Alliance of the Forest People "represents a fundamental step toward preservation of the Amazon by its own inhabitants who seek a new form of using the forest's resources without doing away with forests and their people... The proposals set forth by the Alliance of the Forest People manage to reconcile apparently incompatible things such as: the struggle for better living and working conditions, organization of labor unions, followed by community education and health programs, and the organization of producers' cooperatives. All this based on a greater fight aimed at preservation of an asset that belongs to all the inhabitants of the planet, those already here and the generations yet to come".

(MENDES, Chico. *O Seringueiro* – from a paper published by the National Rubber Tappers' Council).

Previous page:
"Amazonian Aerial Plants Project" - a day in the tree tops photographing orchids, bromeliads, and other epiphytes. The picture shows photographer Leonide Principe and researcher Jefferson da Cruz, the project's scientific consultant, in a *sumaumeira**. The project is sponsored by the Amazonas state government.

Notes from the expeditions' log book:
"During the brief resting periods in my climb up the trunk to reach the tree top, a strange feeling took possession of me. What I felt was respect for that monument nature had created – the same respect I had felt during storms at sea or when standing at the edge of a great waterfall. Viewing the landscape from such a vantage point is an extraordinary experience.
The solid slender trunk drew a definite outline in my mind's eye. The branches jutted out on all sides like a giant canopy. My companions who stood at the foot of the tree were seen as tiny dots, just heads and arms...
... Wanting to associate this experience to memories of my boyhood, to countless days of tree-climbing, I might even be able to find the same enthusiasm, the same adventurous impulse. But in adulthood, tree-climbing is somehow quite different. I would even go so far as to say that there is a rational presence in the forest, something living, an essence that goes beyond my comprehension.
There is life in the forest, something that our civilization has lost sight of. This makes me feel that expeditions to environments that feature wildlife are intrinsic to my work; like the perfumed essence of orchids, they carry me to a more subtle and volatile plane. These expeditions take me to a borderless frontier, beyond concrete knowledge and mere textbook learning."

The future

Foreign tourists dive into Lake Janauacá. The
forest, inhospitable and wild, becomes a tropical
paradise, one stage of an exotic vacation.

The meeting of the waters: the Negro River on the left, and the Solimões River on the right — the beginning of the Amazon River.

An Amazon Civilization

History is demonstrating that people can play the main role in their own destiny against the manipulators and speculators that seek to draw the course of this trail in their own favor. We cannot allow any lack of hope for a better world, exactly now when the first shy attempts at a new way of thinking are beginning to appear.

Reality is the fruit of thoughts and actions. If the dominating thought is led to see the bad side of things, this is generally reflected on the geographical, social, and individual landscapes. But if greenery invades people's thoughts and if only half of the population were to plant a tree each month, how many more trees would we have by the end of each year?

Meeting of the waters of the Branco River, lower left, and the Negro River, above.

Relevant sectors of the great world businesses, at times the very ones that were responsible for the degradation, are sniffing out the potential of a new green market. Any company that is behind the times on this issue will be decreeing its own end. "Sustainable development" is a magic expression agreeable to many. It represents the capacity to reach a satisfactory level of development by using natural resources without affecting the ecosystems.

Now more than ever, mass media must redeem its educational task, directing society toward the solution of problems. The Brazilian and international press associated the Amazon forest with man's destructive actions. Within the mass communication media it is difficult to find any example of articles on the Amazon that do not show burning off, deforestation, *garimpeiros** using mercury, sick Indians, murdered *seringueiros**, and the degraded environ-

Moon over the Amazon River.

Otters (*Pteonura brasiliensis*) live in groups swimming in the rivers and often making a great deal of noise. They are excellent swimmers and dive to catch fish which they carry away to eat on land.

This otter is endemic to South America and is the largest of the sixty-three species of the Mustelidae family. It ranks at the top of the pyramid of predators with the jaguar, anaconda, and the crested eagle. It has no natural enemies.

There are many groups of otters on the Xixuaú-Xiparinã Reservation (Jauaperi River – Roraima). The *Associação Amazônia* is responsible for administration of the reservation.

ment. Unfortunately, all of this does exist, but the insistence on looking only at this has contributed to create a state of suspicion and hostility that perpetuates the decadent condition of the Amazon people. This people has not yet managed to become fully aware of the great value of the unlimited potential of its region, in every sense.

This is the largest forest in the world, unique in size and density. It holds the largest reserves of fresh water on the planet, and the greatest natural gene bank that contains precious data on life's adaptation to the most diverse situations.

We note how important all this is when we

look at the first map of the earth based on satellite photographs, a map made by the American artist Tom Van Sant, and NASA engineer Lloyd Van Warren. The Amazon appears in the planet's most extensive and most intense green, testifying to a vocation that must be considered, in the first place, by its own inhabitants. It is obvious that this faithful image of the earth points to the Amazon. It is obvious that the Amazon has something very special that led it to be the focal point of attention throughout the world.

Development and awareness of a genuinely Amazonian people must be encouraged. This people will show all other nations that here there is something unique and irreplaceable, and that all must contribute to its preservation. The ready availability of natural resources applied to the benefit of the Amazon people, without

Peixes-boi* (*Trichechus inunguis*). Shy, tame, and slow aquatic mammals, the *peixes-boi** are on the official list of endangered Brazilian species, classified as vulnerable by the World Conservation Union – IUCN. They are endemic to the Amazon region, and occur in the Amazon River and its tributaries, even to the point where the Amazon empties into the Atlantic Ocean. When hunted, they become cautious, and as they have very keen senses, it becomes difficult to capture them. When chased, they dive and stay under water for quite some time. However, as the mammals that they are, they must renew the air in their lungs, but they show only their snouts when they sense man's presence.

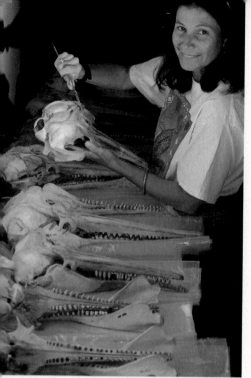

Researcher Vera M. F. da Silva, of the INPA* Aquatic Mammals Laboratory, measuring and cataloging *boto vermelho* (*Inia geoffrensis*) skulls.

degradation of the ecosystems, would certainly be a more sensible alternative means of inverting the trend that leads to disaster.

The wealth contained in the Amazon is incalculable because this wealth is not merely material: there is an intangible wealth that can never be determined. Attempts to evaluate this wealth, even though only quantitatively, already represent a wider range of natural resources to improve the quality of life of this generation and of those to come in the future. But there are still several mysteries related to the Amazon that constitute a challenge to man. The intangible wealth of the Amazon transcends the guidelines of market economy that

Below: Fernando Rosas, researcher at the INPA* Aquatic Mammals Laboratory, feeding a baby *peixe-boi**.
Right: animal morphology and weighing.

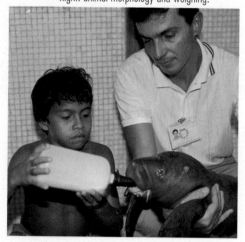

The INPA* *Peixe-boi* Project was created in 1974 to study the biology of this animal that is so little known and already listed as an endangered species, and to draw up measures for its preservation and handling. Every year the Aquatic Mammals Laboratory receives several offspring orphaned due to the illegal hunting that still occurs in the region. Here they are bred on an artificial diet. The first Amazonian *Peixe-boi** conceived in captivity was born twenty-four years after the project's implementation (photo at left). This event gives renewed hope for preservation of the species. The "*Associação Amigos do Peixe-boi*" (Friends of the Peixe-boi Association) was created to encourage the population's greater participation in conservation efforts.

govern human action, because this wealth is related to a spiritual dimension of man's relations with nature.

At present, the European countries, the United States, and Japan, that possess advanced technology, are more concerned about environmental issues. The Amazon may be the synthesis of food for humanity, the synthesis of need-

ed medicaments, the synthesis of fresh water, the synthesis of biodiversity of the future, the synthesis of the lost paradise that must be re-conquered...

All must contribute to the birth of this new Amazon civilization, a civilization that should be characterized as the refuge of world ecology. It is the respected habitat of biodiversity, God's great work that cannot be lost. The people of the Amazon will have to administer it wisely with worldwide support. Finally and above all, although retaining its national identity, the Amazon must be considered a natural asset of all humankind.

On the right:
Sumaumeira* (*Ceiba pentandra*). Iara and Carlo, on a visit to the Amazon, admire the majestic *sumaumeira**; an opportunity to reflect on Nature's great works.

Bruce Nelson, INPA* Botanic Department researcher collecting plant species.

William Magnuson, INPA* Biology Department researcher, photographing a snake.

174

On the right:
Cachoeira Santuário
(Santuário Waterfall),
on the road between
Presidente Figueiredo
and the Balbina dam.

INPA* researcher Roger Cribel
and his assistant, Aldenora,
carrying out field research on
pollination of the *sumaumeira**
(*Ceiba pentandra*) flowers.

Xingu River — *Pedra da Caxinguba* (Caxinguba Rock)

Low relief of the Pedra da Caxinguba highlighted in chalk by researcher Victor Py-Daniel.

Flock of Great Egrets in flight.

A Great Challenge

Our desire is that the Amazon cease to be a forest in flames. Our desire is that it be the only great forest that humanity managed to preserve, where the people who inhabit it fulfill the mission of guarding the precious vault of nature. The Amazon forest is the most important capital of all races: the true "World Bank". A bank that in the near future

Researcher Roger William
Hutchings collecting butterflies
in the Pico da Neblina region.

181

The 1st Brazilian Multi-disciplinary and Multi-institutional Expedition to the Pico da Neblina in 1990. The expedition was organized and coordinated by INPA*, the Brazilian armed forces (army and air force), and various Brazilian research institutes (UNISINOS; FZB-RS; UFPr; FIOCRUZ). The expedition included inland-water geoscientists, zoologists, botanists, and geologists. The main object was to collect zoological, botanical and geological data and material from two specific areas: the region of the *Morro dos Seis Lagos*, and that of the Pico da Neblina itself. Publication of a large volume of scientific data is still underway.

Climbing the Pico da Neblina.

will pardon all debts of those who degraded and wasted its natural resources. Then the old and luxuriant green mantle can be redeemed over the whole of the planet's surface.

Humanity faces a great challenge: the commitment of all those who concern themselves with environmental issues and who are willing to bet on man's capacity to revert the disastrous tendency of our time. There is a legend that says that on the occasion of a great forest fire, all the animals seek to escape. Only one little humming bird was gathering a few drops of water from the river and flying high to drop them on the fire. They asked the humming bird what use was it to do so little.

And the humming bird answered:

"If everyone were to do just a little..."

Arrival at the peak of Pico da Neblina (3,014 m), the highest point in Brazil.

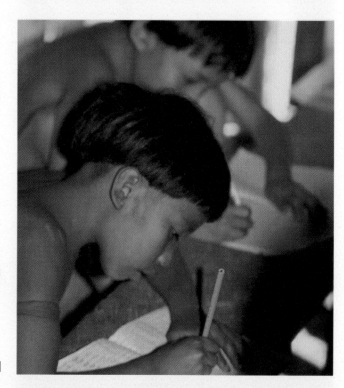

Health and social assistance for the Amazon Indians.
Services rendered by the GAP *Congregação das Irmãs da Providência* (Sisters of Providence) in Xitei/Xidea (Yanomami area) in Roraima are an example of activities directly aimed at the human being.
"Land and Self-Sustenance: helping the Yanomami to perceive the vulnerability of their autonomy in view of inevitable contact with the surrounding society, and to strengthen their self-sustenance".
"Health: promoting life by providing immediate and ongoing care of the ill, fighting to achieve all-round health for the Yanomami through the use of preventive and remedial medicine.
"Education: aiming at global and liberating education with emphasis on the training of student-teachers capable of building up specific and differentiated teaching methods to prepare the Yanomami to actively and creatively overcome impacts stemming from the surrounding society (awareness building)".

184

Aerial view of the *Morro dos 6 Lagos* (6-Lake Hill).

INPA* Researcher Victor Py-Daniel, measuring the level of radioactivity on the *Morro dos 6 Lagos* which features deposits of various radioactive minerals. Among these is niobium, used mainly by the aeronautics and astronautics industries. The region's reserves of this mineral are said to be among the largest in the world.

185

Caboclo* child playing
with a *bicho-pau*.

Humanity is facing a great challenge:

– to make peace with the environment;
– to observe nature's wisdom;
– to enrich itself with diversity.

Aerial view of Janauari Park. In the upper right-hand corner, the city of Manaus.

Ariaú Amazon Towers — The observation towers of the jungle hotel provide a panoramic view of the forest. From the tower one can observe life in the tree tops, birds in flight, the *igapós**, the Negro River, and the islands of the Anavilhanas archipelago.

Epilogue

Previous page:
Aerial view of the Ariaú
Amazon Towers.

Foreign tourist
photographing Amazon
water lilies (*vitória-régia**)
on Janauacá Lake.

Yachtsman Thierry van Erseel on
a trip to Amazonas, playing with
a wooly monkey (*Lagothrix
lagothricha*).

The Amazon always constituted a fascinating attraction to humanity and it allows no indifference: it inspires both adoration and terror, dividing the opinions of wise men and intellectuals throughout the ages.

At the start of this century, there were two distinct lines of thought in nearly everything that was written or thought about the Amazon. On one hand, the "infernists" defined the Amazon as an unknown and dangerous place. The terror is explicit in literature of that time. From there comes the expression "green hell" used in novels by Alberto Rangel, in accounts by Euclides da Cunha and in *Cobra Norato*, the most important work of Raul Bopp. The other line of thought, that of the "edenists" such as Pereira da Silva, author of *Poemas Amazônicos*, maintained that the Amazon represented a true paradise. To them, Nature, in all its glory, was the personification of creation.

Throughout the centuries, thousands of adventurers and conquistadors were defeated by the forest which defended itself against invaders with its size plus the heat and humidity of the tropics, the courage of the Indian warriors, the enormous and solitary beasts like the jaguars, or tiny swarming insects like the *caba**. The impertinence of invading and the pretentiousness of thinking they could domesticate the jungle already cost many lives and caused many disillusions.

The Amazon also helped to enhance the feats of boasters avid for heroic laurels.

In the modern world, movies and television disseminated the Amazon's reputation as a hostile environment. This fiction, supported by all the

Tourists observing a small amphibian during an excursion promoted by Ariaú Towers.

Tourist outing to the forest.

resources available to exhibit illusion, populated the Amazon environment with horrendous monsters. Audiences the world over were chilled by the sight of murderous *piranhas*, terrifying spiders, enormous snakes, and other "Amazon" creatures invented by the talent and technology of modern cinema. The sensationalist press and mass media throughout the world also multiplied their profits by airing news about accidents and catastrophes. All this stimulates the exaggerations of newscasts featuring burning, deforestation, the massacre of Indians, pollution of rivers, and so much other "information" about the destruction of the "lungs of the world".

Unknown and mysterious, the Amazon also stirred an overwhelming interest in Jacques Cousteau, the most famous maker of documentaries on nature of all times. I met him in 1982 when he was a guest at the Mônaco Hotel in Manaus for thirteen months, and where he set up

This plant, known here as the "moon cactus" (*Strophocactus wittii*), is a rare species native to the Negro River. It was long sought after by the famous English artist Margaret Mee who drew the cactus flower.

Fishing *piramutaba**,
one of the Amazonian catfish.

the base of his operations to document life in the planet's largest forest.

During this period, we met frequently in the hotel's penthouse restaurant where we had the opportunity to talk at length, inspired by the view: on one side, the grand Teatro Amazonas standing out from the backdrop of the city. and on the other, the immense Bay of the Negro River joining the silhouette of the forest to mark the line of the horizon.

This peaceful atmosphere was not immune to the great threat hovering over the early '80s: that of a nuclear war. I was very interested in hearing Cousteau's opinion on this matter. After having passed sixteen years of my life in the infantry of the Brazilian army and in the Jungle War Instruction Center, military surroundings, I was uneasy about the dread of an international conflict of unimaginable proportions, I was faced with a man confident that peace would reign. He expressed his tranquility by searching the depths of the seven seas to show the harmony of nature in the cradle of life: the water.

With the experience and wisdom of one who had carried out research on lands and people of five continents, Commander Jacques Cousteau had already seen presidents of many countries, intellectuals, artists, religious leaders, scientists, people from all over the world concerned about the cold war. However, he himself was convinced that the danger was on another front.

At a time when words such as environment and ecology were not yet in style, Cousteau assured me that the main threat to humanity's survival was the destruction of nature. That dreaded nuclear war,

The Boa Vida jungle hotel.

capable of destroying the whole planet, would not happen because the men who had the power to detonate the atomic bombs would also die. And they had no desire to commit suicide.

The wise commander of the Calypso, the famous laboratory-yacht anchored in the waters of the Negro River Bay, warned that ongoing destruction of the Amazon could cause another conflict. According to Cousteau, if this destruction is not halted by the year 2000, everyone will be compromising the survival of his or her chil-

The Amazon Lodge jungle hotel.

Araujo, Captain Barata, is a *caboclo** typical of those who work in the tourist trade. A knowledgeable woodsman, he demonstrates how to extract water from a liana. Forest dwellers use this liana, known to them as the "water liana", to quench their thirst.

dren, grandchildren, and great grandchildren. So, either we must preserve the Amazon, or it will somehow be defended by other nations. There could be attempts at military occupation, or the forestlands might be purchased. In any case, something will be done to prevent desperation when humanity becomes aware that the life of its descendents is at stake.

With all the burning, the genetic resources of the Amazon, still to be studied, could turn to ash. The Amazon biodiversity, considering only its potential for cures, represents a treasure greater than all its other natural reserves, including minerals and timber, which are the largest and most coveted in the world. Fully twenty-five percent of all the pharmaceutical essences used in medicine were extracted from tropical forests. They include quinine that has been used to treat malaria for nearly 100 years, or vincristine and vimblastine, chemotherapeutic drugs used to fight cancer. The leaves of the *jaborandi**, a bush that grows

199

nowhere else in the world but in certain areas of the Amazon, yield polycarpine to produce eye drops used against glaucoma, a disease that can lead to blindness. To treat high blood pressure, medicaments are made from the poison of the *jararaca* or pit viper, an Amazonian snake that reduces the blood pressure of its prey to zero. And very little is as yet known about the proliferation of life in the Amazon forest where it is estimated that more than two million species live. Only in the small space occupied by a footprint

Caboclo* with his finished handicraft, a piece representing a pirarucu*.

made by the sole of a shoe up to 1,500 live species can be counted, including fungi and microorganisms. Just imagine what can be found in the 6.5 million square kilometers that make up the continental Amazon region, an area greater than the whole of Europe, excluding what was previously the Soviet Union.

Floating tourist site on Janauri Lake.

From these conversations with Jacques Cousteau I came to perceive that the most important people of the planet would need and want to become acquainted with the Amazon, to feel it and to see it with their own eyes.

Thus was born the idea of building a small hotel in the middle of the forest to be able to show people what the virgin forest, untouched by man, is really like.

Before choosing the site where I was to build the hotel, I wanted to better understand the wishes of people who visited the Amazon. To this end, besides lots of conversations with

Amazon Village jungle hotel.

201

Igarapé – A ray of sunlight in the forest and the golden water of the springs.

dozens of tourists, I made a survey that greatly helped me get to know about the wants and interests of visitors.

Taking a boat trip on the great rivers of the Amazon was one of the dreams of tourists. More than 2,000 species of fish live in these rivers.

To set up the hotel, I chose the region of the Ariaú *Paraná* which forms a secret connection between the Negro and Solimões rivers. These two rivers come together in the famous meeting of the waters to form the Amazon River, the second

largest river in the world with 5,904 kilometers in length. The waters of these two
gigantic rivers flow through the Ariaú
Paraná*, thirty miles from Manaus which
one can now cover in an hour by boat
traveling north on the Negro River. It is a
region that to this day could be described
by the "edenists" of the early 1900s as the
lost paradise. There, nature's supreme
exuberance induces city dwellers to a state
of contemplation that produces an inde-
scribable well being. Some say it makes
them feel younger, energizing them with
the forces of nature in its purest state.
Others attempt to describe the emotion of
their deepest encounters with their own
inner self and with the universe. There
each one lives his or her own experience in
an unparalleled manner. Today, when I
leaf through the guest books where
60,000 visitors have registered their opinions, I find that all tend to summarize
their descriptions with one sole word:
wonderful, written in languages as different as Chinese, Polish, or Arabic.

Once the site was chosen, it was necessary to
face the challenge of building the hotel without
disturbing the forest. Our proposal was to adapt
the hotel to the forest in such a way that the instal-
lations could be built without felling one sole tree.
And we managed. In the beginning there were
only four suites. Today it is a complex of 220
suites with the comfort and safety necessary to
allow the unforgettable experience of sleeping in

Guests of the Ariaú Towers during the sighting of alligators. Carlo, a courageous boy, holds a baby alligator that will be freed immediately following observation.

Iara, a young and kindly tourist with a common squirrel monkey (*Saimiri sciureus*).

the middle of the forest. Occupying the rare empty spaces in the jungle, we built six wooden towers interconnected by raised walkways so guests walk among the treetops. The walkways connect the towers that house the guest suites, restaurants, auditoriums, library, and the facilities that allow strolls in the company of monkeys and coatis, similar to the raccoon but with a longer snout and tail. These animals are becoming increasingly intimate with hotel guests.

Life in the treetops is a surprisingly intense and beautiful experience. It is there that the macaws make their nests, where many orchids bloom. Butterflies, bromeliads and some thousands of other animals and plants of all shapes and colors form a chain in an ecosystem that fascinates observers. Apart from the walkways, people's dreams of integrating themselves in this aerial world encouraged me to build the Tarzan's house, a comfortable suite installed in the uppermost branches of a Brazil nut tree at a height of 36 meters. It is the preferred accommodations for celebrities of the entertainment industry – cinema and show business. On the other hand, leading politicians of some countries and directors of multinational corporations induced me to build a "cosmic suite", an area comprising 200 square meters with a representation of the universe and its stars. Equipped with all the instruments of modern computer technology and communications, the "cosmic suite" allows visitors to be constantly on-line, via Internet, with their own world and with the rest of the world. From the powerful guests of the "cosmic suite", I began to understand that there are people who can never remain isolated. At times they must get away from their own environment to study complex processes and allow important decisions to mature. "You have to get away from the mountain in order to see it" say the wise men, kings, and presidents.

Instead of the contrast between primitive nature and the modernity of a large spatial suite equipped with computers and telephones, the Ariaú Towers also receives guests who prefer to meditate tuning in to the forces of the universe by means of the energy of the pyramids and crystals. That is why the Ariaú Towers also features a transparent pyramid with the same proportions, and placed in the same orientation relative to the sun as the famous and mysterious Egyptian Khufu (or Cheops) pyramid near Giza.

Those who return to the

On the preceding page: Aerial view of the Ariaú Amazon Towers jungle hotel. On the left-hand side of the photo one sees the regional boat that goes back and forth between the hotel and Manaus cutting through the waters of the Negro River. On the right-hand side is the Ariaú *paraná**, the starting point for canoe trips that allow tourists from all over the world to discover the Amazon universe of lakes, with their *furos**, *igapós**, *igarapés**, the native inhabitants, and rich plant life, Many of these tourists register their impressions in the hotel's guest book with promises of future visits, while others simply enthuse about this mythical Eden.

Little Luna looking at the delicate squirrel monkey.

Ariaú Towers are generally surprised at the new spaces whatever they may be: a wild orchid nursery, a pool alongside the tree tops, a convention hall, or an UFO landing strip, our UFO-port. But that is the way of the Ariaú Towers, always undergoing evolution. It is not a work subject to any definite timeframe for conclusion, but one subject to ongoing improvement with the commitment of making any stay an incomparably agreeable one for all the hotel's guests, be they a pleasant modest couple living in Manaus, a rich and famous group of artists, politicians, or businessmen from all parts of the world. For all of these reasons, the Ariaú Towers has been the theme of extensive reports published by the most important and influential regional, national, and international communications media: *Rede Amazônica*, *Rede Calderaro de Comunicação*, *Rede Globo* and its famous programs *Fantástico*, *Globo Ecologia*, *Globo Repórter*... The newspapers *Folha de São Paulo*, *Gazeta Mercantil*, *Jornal do Brasil*; magazines *Viagem*, *IstoÉ*, *Manchete*; *Editora Abril* and its prestigious magazines *Veja*, *Playboy*, *Quatro Rodas*, *Superinteressante*, *Caminhos da Terra*, *Elle*, *Cláudia*... *National Geographic*, *Travel Tour News*, *Town & Country*, *InViaggio*... There are so many that it is impossible to mention all.

NewsWeek, internationally acknowledged as one of the magazines of greatest penetration throughout the world, published an article in its August/08/98 issue

The Pyramid and the UFO-port at the Araiú Amazon Towers.

that included the Ariaú Towers among the seven wonders of the world: "on this earth, one of the only remaining intact destinies for your next vacation". This respectful treatment and the generous compliments the Ariaú Towers has received from all the press professionals throughout the world have increased our responsibility toward Amazon ecotourism and further cemented our commitments to Nature. This Amazonian Nature is what has taught us to remain humble and to carry on our job of defending it.

It is in harmony with this Amazonian Nature that we wish you a hearty welcome to the Amazon.

On the right:
Adult sloth with baby (Bradypus tridactylus).
Sloths spend most of their lives in trees, descending to the ground
only to move from one tree to another. The imbaubeira (tree of
the Moraceae family – Cecropia genus) is held to be the sloths'
main source of food, but contrary to common belief, sloths feed
on hundreds of different species of trees. This keeps them
constantly on the move and proves that they are not at all lazy,
as their name implies, besides showing that there is nothing
wasteful about their feeding habits.

"We're not lazy, but highly
sensitive" – Phrase uttered by
Heidi Mosbark, German
researcher who dedicated more
than twenty years to studying
sloths. She died in 1998 after
having lived all those years in
isolation at the headwaters of
the Cuieiras River.

These two pages are a way of
rendering our modest homage to
this unique and altruistic woman.

Glossary

Açaí – (*Euterpe precatoria* and *Euterpe oleracea* – from the Tupi *yasa'i*, the fruit that weeps.) A palm that grows in clumps in damp soil, producing large bunches of burgundy colored fruit throughout the year from which a delicious rich juice is made. One variety's juice is greenish in color. To make the juice, it is advisable to leave the fruit soaking for some time in warm water to facilitate peeling.

Acará – (The most common genus is the *Geophagus* spp.). This is the generic name for the Cichlids, a large family of fish common to the whole of the Amazon region.

Amapá – (*Brosimum parinarioide* – from the indigenous Tupi word *amapá*). A tree of the Moraceae family, which has good wood and from whose bark is extracted a milky liquid that has medicinal properties. The people in the Amazon use this to treat asthma, bronchitis and other respiratory tract disorders; used externally, it promotes formation of scar tissue.

Anta – (*Tapirus terrestris* – from the Tupi *tapi'ra*). A synonym for tapir. A large mammal found in the wet forests of South America. The adult can reach as much as 2 meters in length and 1 meter in height. It feeds on forest grasses, fruits and flowers. Its natural predators are the *onça** (*Panthera onca*) and possibly the large *sucurijus*, the anacondas. Due to its abundant and excellent meat, it is the frequent quarry of hunters and is in danger of becoming extinct.

Arari – A small Amazon scaled fish with a red tail, reaching about 20cms in length, little used for human food but, as a lower link in the natural underwater food chain, eagerly sought by larger fish.

Arroz-de-marreca – (*Oryza* spp.). Literally, "duck rice". A grass commonly found in Amazon lakes having the interesting characteristic of growing straight up, along with the flooding, to reach heights of over 6 meters. It produces rice similar to the commonly known variety (*Oryza sativa*), but 90% or more without grains. There is intense life in the rice paddies, both on the surface and underwater, as numerous birds and fish feed on this grain.

Aruanã – (*Osteoglossum ferrerae*) The Black Aruana. A scaled fish that can grow to a meter in length and physically resembles the *pirarucu** slightly. It lives in *igapós** and lakes and basically feeds on insects and small fish. Thanks to its habit of always swimming on the surface, it is easily shot with a bow and arrow or speared using an *azagaia**.

Azagaia – A trident fitted to a wooden shaft for nocturnal fishing using a *poronga** or lantern.

Bacaba – (*Oenocarpus bacaba* – from the Tupi *wa'kawa*). A palm tree bearing large bunches of fruit from which a highly nutritive, ochre colored, juice is extracted. The method of extracting the juice is the same as that used for *açaí**. Cultivated rationally on an industrial scale, it yields excellent heart of palm, as do many of the Amazon palm trees.

Balateiro – A person who exploits the balata, a tree that grows on dry land and which apart from having good wood, also yields latex used as the raw material to make chewing gum.

Barracão – In this context, refers to the warehouse in which the rubber plantation owner stores provisions received from town that are supplied to rubber-tappers.

Beiju – A kind of flat, round cake made from grated cassava or tapioca flour. It is made in the same oven after drying the flour, or in a frying pan on an open fire and is seasoned with salt and sometimes with pieces of Brazil nut. There are several ways to prepare it amongst which "beijucica". In this form, it is dried and lasts longer.

Beiradão – A word used by the river dwellers to indicate the riverbanks, the higher parts on the sides of large Amazon rivers where they build their houses.

Bicho-folha and Bicho-pau – Stick and leaf Insects. Insects that resemble twigs or leaves and which, by a form of "congenital mimicry", take on features of their habitat as a means of protection from predators.

Boto vermelho – (*Inia geoffrensis*). Cetacean living in Amazon rivers and lakes. Its behavior is similar to that of dolphins. One of the most common legends referring to the animal is that it changes into a well-dressed, handsome young man who goes to parties along the river where he seduces the girls. Before dawn, he runs off and returns to the river or lake where he changes back into a *boto**. On his expedition, Jacques Cousteau gave it the "pink" denomination. In Amazon tradition, however, it is known as the "red" *boto**. It tends to roam singly or in pairs and frequently approaches man, even when fishing. The other *boto**, the *tucuxi** (*Sotalia fluviatilis*), has a darker back and is smaller. It is shyer and is habitually seen in pods, even when not in the mating season. The text contains more information on the *boto**.

Branquinha – (Cichlid Family: 6 genera). Smaller fish than the *jaraqui**, although similar in appearance except for their coloration, which is completely white. After reproducing, they gather preferably in lakes.

Caba – Great variety of hornets of the wasp family whose stings are extremely painful.

Cabeceira – In rivers and black-water lakes, these are channels that cut into the land and are larger than the *igarapés**, on occasion many kilometers long. However, they do not sustain life in that, as a general rule, they end (or begin) in a simple spring. Not to be confused with the homograph *cabeceira** – the source of a river or *igarapé**.

Caboclo – The Amazon region river dweller. Brown skinned, fruit of centuries of miscegenation between the native Indians and many other folk – principally Brazilians from the Northeast, Portuguese, Bolivians, Peruvians, Colombians, Syrians, Lebanese and Jews – pioneers from the time prior to the rubber boom, or who took part in the boom. Over time, the caboclos absorbed the millenarian wisdom derived from many indigenous ethnic groups.

Cacau – (*Theobroma cacau*). Chocolate is produced from the seeds of this fruit. A lighter colored chocolate is also made from the seeds of its less sophisticated "cousin", the *cupuaçu**.

Canarana – (*Paspalum* spp. and *Panicum* spp.) A grass that grows on the edges of rivers, lakes and *paranás**. It grows so well in the muddy waters (rich in mineral nutrients) that it can block the mouths of lakes and *paranás** (blockages), hampering navigation. It is the most easily available fodder for cattle confined on *marombas**.

Capivara – (*Hydrochoerus hydrochaeris*). The largest of all rodents. They live in bands on the edge of rivers, lakes and *igarapés**, feed mainly on grasses and wild fruits, and are adroit at swimming and diving. If it weren't for their extraordinary reproductive ability, they would also be facing extinction.

Casco – A canoe made of a single tree trunk, first hollowed out using ax and adze and then further widened by fire. The *casco* is different from the Indian *ubá*, which is merely scraped out and not widened and thus less pot-bellied and stable. Not to be confused with the igarité (see entry in this glossary), which is a larger canoe fitted with protective decking that can be used for cargo and for transporting people on short journeys.

Castanha – In this context we refer to the "castanha-do-pará", the Brazil nut which is a valuable food, the fruit of a tree of the same name,

(*Bertholletia excelsa*), one of the largest and most beautiful trees on dry land in the Amazon forest.

Castanheira – (*Bertholletia excelsa*), one of the largest and most beautiful trees on dry land in the Amazon forest. See the entry for *Castanha*.

Caucho – (*Castiloa ulei* - from *kautchuk*, a word in the indigenous language spoken along the banks of the upper Amazon). A large forest tree growing on dry land from which latex, inferior in quality to that of the *seringueira**, is bled. See the entry for *Balateiro*, in this glossary.

Cebolinha and Cheiro-verde – Indispensable herbs for the *caldeiradas** (stew) - (fresh fish simmered in a plentiful broth), that the *caboclo** grows in suspended beds, generally made from old canoes.

Charuto – (*Leporellus cartledgei*) A tasty scaled fish of the Characidae, having an almost chubby body, 20 to 25 centimeters in length. It is found in rivers and lakes and usually caught using a throw net.

Cobra-grande – A huge legendary snake that inhabits steep underwater riverbanks in eddies where rivers and *igarapés** meet.

Coirão – A coarse word, used to ridicule persons.

Colocação – A location chosen by the *seringueiro**, most frequently in the bush, as a point of departure for *seringa** trails, where latex is collected and where the latex is then smoked late in the afternoon.

Coronel – A respectful designation for the *seringalista** who provides basic supplies and controls the *seringueiro's* life. In the past, the Government granted these traders the rank of colonel in the National Guard. A disparagement: in the Amazon region – *coronel-de-barranco*; in the Northeast – *coronel-rabo-de-cabra*.

Cubiu – (*Tetragonopterus argenteus* - from the Tupi *kubi'u*) A fish with features resembling the *charuto* (See entry in this glossary.)

Cuia – A gourd, fruit of the *cuieira* (*Crescentia cujete*). In general, these are sawn in half, and the pulp is removed. The halves are then used as small basins to hold flour, bail water from a dugout canoe, etc. Also known as *cabaça* or *coité*. Plastic or tin recipients are gradually taking the place of the cuia, and there is thus less incentive to plant it.

Cunhã – (from the Tupi *ku'ña*) An Indian woman.

Cunhantã – An adolescent Indian girl.

Cupuaçu – (*Theobroma grandiflorum* - from the Tupi , large *cupu*). A medium sized tree widely cultivated by *caboclos**. The fruit of this tree –

a large pod containing seeds and a tasty aromatic pulp – is used to make sweets and juices. See the entry for *Cacau*, in this glossary.

Curimatá – (*Prochilodus* spp. - from the Tupi *kuruma'tá*). A scaled white fish of the Characidae family, that measures about 30 cm, feeds on slime and mud, and whose preferred habitat is lakes and *paranás**. It is caught with a throw net or conventional nets.

Curumim – An Indian and by extension, a *caboclo** boy.

Defumação – When the *seringueiro** arrives back from his latex collecting, he makes a very smoky fire (preferably using the *ouricuri* coconut) and, slowly pours the latex through the smoke using a stake, to form the *pela** (ball), the first process the rubber undergoes.

Envira – A fiber extracted from the bark of several trees to make string or ropes, or simply just to tie up something.

Estrada de seringa – The *seringueiro** makes long trails in the forest, between the sparsely distributed *seringueiras** to mark and find his way back and forth in collecting latex.

Facheação – Nocturnal fishing with an *azagaia**, using a lantern or torch.

Furo – An opening carved by the water between trees in the *igapó**. During the flood season, such openings allow the passage of small vessels and canoes, shortening the distance between lakes, *paranás** and rivers. In some communities *furos* are made with machetes, always with the intention of shortening the path. In the dry season, these openings turn into foot paths.

Garimpeiro – An person who works as a prospector.

Garimpo – In the Amazon region, there are land-based prospecting sites (where gold nuggets, diamonds, other precious stones, and innumerable minerals are sought) and alluvial prospecting sites on the banks and in the beds of rivers, *paranás** and *igarapés**, from which the gold powder, leached out by the torrents, is extracted. All these processes are highly predatory and cause irreparable damage to the environment. Alluvial prospecting is the most pernicious: besides damaging the river banks and destroying all the flora encountered there, it also pollutes the waters and so extinguishes fish and reptile life and, also by extension, that of the immense variety of river birds. All this without taking into account the silting-up and the harm caused by mercury used to separate the mineral.

Grileiro – A person who takes possession of, makes use of, or sets up on another's land. *Grileiros* sometimes obtain false deeds, simply refuse to move, or even sells the land, thereby creating legal problems.

Guaraná – (*Paullinia cupana* - from the Tupi *waráná*). A large Amazon forest vine, cultivated by the Saterê-Maués Indians, the pods of which provide seeds rich in stimulant substances, such as caffeine. The seeds are roasted and then ground to powder, under a mortar. Water is added slowly until a consistent paste is formed which is transformed into a bar, known as a *guaraná* "cake". The bony tongue of the *pirarucu** is used to grate the cake and prepare a soft drink that prevents drowsiness in those engaged in nocturnal activities. It is also an aphrodisiac, stomachic, keeps up the strength of those walking long distances, and when taken in small amounts, benefits the cardiovascular system.

Igapó – (from the Tupi *ia'pó*). A stretch of forest having its own vegetation, through which the waters normally penetrate during the flood season. Many varieties of fish depend on the *igapós** to spawn, and to protect and feed their fry. In general, the aquatic life of the Amazon basin is very dependent on the *igapós** because of the fruit, insects, and small animals they contain. Therefore, to maintain ecological balance, it is essential that the vegetation of the flooded areas be preserved.

Igarapé – (from the Tupi *ïara'pé*, a water way). Small river, a canoe route.

Igarité – (from the Tupi *iari'té*, a real canoe). See entry for *Casco*, in this glossary.

INPA – Amazon Region National Research Institute. As a Ministry of Science and Technology center of excellence, the Institute's primary objective is to investigate the environment and provide interactive solutions for humans to use in the Amazon region. In producing the photographs and texts for this book, the help and support received from INPA was not only considerable, but fundamental to conclusion of this project.

Jaborandi – (*Pilocarpus jarborandi* - from the Tupi *yaborá'di*). A bush whose leaves and pods have medicinal effects. Pilocarpine is extracted from these parts of the tree.

Jacundá – (*Crenicichla* spp.). The generic name for a great variety of fish of the Cichlid family. The *jacundá*, which has features similar to those of the *tucunaré**, is very skilled at hiding among roots or in holes in the trunks of submerged trees and stones, making it difficult for the torch light bearer to catch him.

Jaraqui – (*Semaprochilodus insignis* and *S. xaenuirus* – from the Tupi *yara'ki*) – An extremely tasty fish of the Characidae family, very common in the Amazon region, and which, together with manioc meal, constitutes the basic diet of the lower income brackets population.

Jaú – (*Paulicea lütkeni'* - from the Tupi *ya'ú*). A fish of the Pimelodidae family. One of the largest scaleless fish in Brazil. In its adult form, it can reach 1.5 meters in length and 120 kg in weight.

Jeju – (*Hoplerythrinus unitaeniatus* - from the Tupi *ye'yu*). Fish of the Characidae family with similar features to the *traíra**. It is extraordinarily resistant to lack of oxygen and can cover dozens of meters slithering like a snake in its search for water when the lake in which it was living dries up completely.

Juta – (*Corchorus capsularis*). Jute, a plant of the Tiliaceae family that originated in India. Its stems produce excellent fiber. Macerated and cleaned, it is used to make fabrics, burlap bags, and cordage.

Juteiro – A person who plants and works with jute, which is sold by the kilo to the factories.

Malhadeira – A fishing implement, which is sold in the locations where there are fish runs. The *caboclo** weaves it with a strong line and wide mesh, to catch adult *tambaquis** and other medium sized fish. The *malhadeiras* currently manufactured industrially with small mesh are highly predatory as small fish are caught indiscriminately before they have had a chance reproduce.

Maloca – The same as *taba** (- from the Tupi *tawa*), an Indian village. In some regions of Brazil, the old usage of a place in which delinquents and outlaws congregate (a *maloqueiro*: person living in such a place), still prevails – a linguistic vestige of colonial times.

Maromba – A high platform made of planks or tree trunks where the cattle are sheltered during heavy floods. It is also used as a refuge for plants, domestic animals and river dwellers' tools.

Marupiara – A person who is lucky in hunting, fishing, in business and even in amorous adventures.

Matrinxã – (*Brycon* spp.). A fish of the Characidae family. The adult fish measures about 0.35cm, is tasty to eat, usually baked. In the spawning run, they are always fat and well nourished thanks to the abundant food available in the *igapós**. They are taken in large number in nets.

Muri – A common grass on the edges of Amazon rivers and lakes. When full grown, it becomes woody and unsuitable as cattle feed.

Mutá – An improvised rustic platform set up in wild fruit trees, on which the hunter, rifle and torch at hand, awaits his prey at night.

Paca – (*Coelogenis paca*). Medium sized rodent (much smaller than the *capivara**) that feeds on wild fruit and nuts.

Pacu – (*Myleus* spp.). Fish of the Characidae family, in various species, distributed throughout most regions of Brazil. They are omnivorous but feed mainly on insects and wild fruit.

Palafita – A house built on high stilts in lakes and areas prone to heavy flooding. In the meadowlands in the Amazon region, *palafitas* are very common. The word *palafita* refers to the stilts and by extension to the houses.

Panema – The antonym of *marupiara**. A person unsuccessful in hunting, fishing or any other undertaking. There are more than a dozen beliefs as to the cause of this state - *panemice*. These superstitions affect the sufferer who, due to autosuggestion, tends to do a poor job of carrying out his tasks.

Paraná – (from the Tupi *para' ná*, similar to the sea). The branch of a river that feeds water back into the same river downstream or into another river. *Paranás* occur frequently In the Amazon Basin and many of them are densely populated.

Patauá – (*Oenocarpus bataua*). A palm tree whose stone fruit, slightly larger than that of the *bacaba** (See entry), provides an excellent ochre colored juice. Being oleaginous, it is a source of good edible oil.

Peixe-boi – (*Trichechus inunguis*). The manatee, a large aquatic* mammal that feeds on water vegetation such as grasses. It ranks as one of the most endangered species. The *caboclo** "identifies" three different flavors in the meat: that of beef, pork and fish. The INPA (Amazon Region National Research Institute) has been making a huge effort to conserve the species and has been successful in getting them to breed in captivity (one specimen).

Pequiá – (*Caryocar villosum* - from the Tupi *piki'á*). Large tree that bears oily, aromatic fruit.

Piracema – The *piracema* (spawning run) is the period during which several species of fish gather in large shoals and swim upstream to the headwaters to spawn.

Piraíba – (*Brachyplatystoma filamentosum*). A fish of the Pimelodidae family. It is the largest scaleless fresh water fish in the Amazon region, and perhaps in the world. Because it can swallow children, the Tupi Indians gave it its name: *pira* = fish + *iba* = not good. An adult speciman can grow to as much as 3 meters in length and near 200 kg in weight. The flesh is quite tasty.

Piramutaba – (*Brachyplatystoma vaillanti* - from the Tupi *piramu'tawa*). A fish of Pimelodidae family. It is very common in rivers of the Amazon region, similar to the catfish, and makes a tasty meal.

Pirapitinga – (*Piaractus brachipomus*). A fish reminiscent of the *tambaqui**, but smaller and with lighter scales (from which *pitinga*, in Tupi), quite common in rivers and lakes of the Amazon region.

Pirarara – (*Phractocephalus hemilopterus*) A smooth skinned fish (scaleless) of the Pimelodidae family that features a dark dorsal region with yellow stripes along the body. It can reach up to 1.30 meters in length and 0.8 meters in diameter.

Pirarucu – (*Arapaima gigas* - from the Tupi *piraru'ku*, red fish). The largest Brazilian scaled fresh water fish and possibly the largest in the world. This fish is very tasty, rivaling cod. Almost boneless, (only backbone and ribs), it is a meaty fish and is separated into two large flaps which, salted and dried in the sun, are sold at the open-air markets, exported and even smuggled. It is widely consumed by the populace and in hotels. It is also eaten fresh, fried, baked, and in the form of fish croquettes. Its bony tongue is used to grate the *guaraná* cake. Its scales are used as exotic, but very efficient nail files, and are also used to make hand crafted products.

Poronga – A kerosene lamp made of tin fitted with a baffle to avoid dazzling the user, and to prevent the flame from being extinguished. It is used by fishermen when spearing fish with the *azagaia** (see entry for *Facheação*) and by *seringueiros**, who begin tapping the *seringueiras** well before dawn.

Pupunha – Fruit of the *pupunheira* (*Bactris gasipaes*), a small palm tree found throughout the Amazon region. The fibrous, yellow or reddish fruit has an excellent flavor and is highly nutritional. It is also used as a sweet in compotes or pastes. Grown on an industrial scale, it provides heart of palm of an excellent nutritional quality.

Quati – (*Nasua nasua* - from the Tupi *akwa'ti*, pointed nose) – A carnivorous (but also omnivorous) mammal whose reddish color is punctuated by black stripes around the body. It has a long tail and dog-like snout, and is a nimble tree climber, preferring to live in bands.

Rango – Slang meaning the worker's midday or evening meal.

Ribeirinhos – Inhabitants of the banks or bluffs of rivers, lakes and *paranás** in the Amazon region. They live in *palafitas**, because of the heavy flooding. The book's main text contains detailed information on the life of the *ribeirinhos**'.

Roçado – An area of approximately a hectare or slightly more where the *caboclo** farms on a short cycle, concentrating on tubers such as cassava, aipi cassava, yams, sweet potatoes; Cucurbitaceae such as watermelon, melons, pumpkins, and gherkins, as well as papaw, corn, bananas etc.

Sardinha – (*Triporteus* spp.). A delicious, silver scaled fish that can grow to as much as 20 to 25 cm, and is found in the Amazon region rivers, normally in shoals.

Seringalista – The owner of a *seringal* – a stand of wild or cultivated rubber trees (that may be covered by title deeds, or be unoccupied government land that was taken over). The "colonel" who owns the store that supplies the *seringueiro** and controls rubber produced and subsequently sold to traders or exporters from the town.

Seringueira – The tree *Hevea brasiliensis*, from whose latex rubber is produced.

Seringueiro – A person who lives by collecting latex and performing the initial processes on rubber. The topic is widely covered in this book.

Sumaumeira or **Sumaúma** – (*Ceiba pentandra* – from the Tupi *sumáuma*) A large tree of the Bombacaceae Family that features white wood and grows in *igapó** areas or near the *igapós**. The huge trunk is supported by enormous roots, the aerial parts of which (known as *sapopemas*) are used to make rustic tables, wash boards, etc. The fruit, in the form of great capsules, is full of kapok-type fiber used as a stuffing for pillows and other household items. An Amazon legend tells of how *Mapinguari*, an enormous legendary creature that protects the forest, strikes the *sapopemas* strongly. The resulting noise frightens away beasts that prey on other animals and on the forest.

Surubim – (*Pseudoplatystoma faciatum*). A common designation for several fish of the Pimelodidae family: *caparari, pintado**, etc.

Tambaqui – (*Colossoma macropomum*). Fish of the Characidae family that feeds on fruit and seeds from the *igapó** vegetation. Its fine flavor is much appreciated throughout the Amazon region and is the basis for many regional recipes. Because it is so highly prized, ever smaller specimens are being taken (the so-called *ruelos*) prior to completing their reproductive cycle. Predatory fishing has placed it in danger of extinction but there are already lakes in which the river dwellers themselves prohibit fishing to ensure its survival and ongoing reproduction. See the entry for *Pirapitinga**, in this glossary.

Taperebá – (*Spondias lutea*). Also known as the *cajá** (*taperebazeiro, cajazeiro*), a large tree with white, brittle wood that yields deliciously perfumed, yellow stoned fruit that is used in juices and sorbets.

Tartaruga – Here we refer to the *Tartaruga-do-amazonas*, the Amazon turtle (*Podocnemis expansa*), considered the largest fresh water chelonian. In its adult state it reaches a length of almost one meter. Because the meat and eggs (about 300 in each clutch) are good to eat, it has been preyed on since the 16th century and is in danger of becoming extinct, as is the case with other chelonians. IBAMA has been successful in surveillance, collecting and hatching eggs on beaches selected for the eggs to be laid. Apart from man, there are a large number of natural predators such as hawks, piranhas, *traíras** and a large number of Pimelodidae.

Timbó – (*Derris* spp.). A leguminous vine of the large *timbó* family that produces a highly toxic effect on fish. Cut into pieces and macerated, it anesthetizes the fish which are then easily caught. Depending on the quantity used, it can have a lethal effect in lakes because the water is not replenished and thus all the fish it contains gradually die.

Traíra – (*Hoplias* spp.) Characid that lives and reproduces in lakes (and is consequently the fish breeder's great enemy) and measures approximately 30 cm. A voracious feeder, it attacks smaller fish with its sharp teeth. There is also a larger variety, the *trairão* (up to 1 meter in length), that is rarely found in Brazil's extreme north.

Tucumã – (*Astrocaryum aculeatum* and *A. vulgare* – from the Tupi *tuku'ma*). A large palm tree, covered in spikes, which produces a fruit whose yellow, oily mesocarp is greatly appreciated by *caboclos** who eat it with manioc meal. Its macerated leaves provide a resistant fiber (as do those of its tucum "cousin") used to make home crafted *malhadeiras*.

Tucunaré – (*Cichla* spp. – from the Tupi *tukuna'ré*) Fish of the Cichlid family, very common in Amazon region rivers and lakes. The *tambaqui** and *acará-açu* are considered the finest fish for use in fish stews - *caldeiradas**. The varieties that live in black waters grow larger than those in muddy waters with the exception of the *tucunaré-açu*. As they are voracious feeders, they are most commonly caught by using a *currico* - a long line with a double hook fixed to a shiny piece of metal that resembles a small fish. Acculturated Indians and riverside dwellers also use the *pindá-siririca* (or *pinaiauaca*), a long pole with about only 20 cm of line and a hook decorated with a red macaw feather.

Tupi – The principal language of the South American indigenous language groups, spoken throughout the Northern and other regions of

Brazil. In the early days of the colonial period (16th and 17th centuries), the Jesuit priests blended it with *guarani* – a language spoken specifically in the coastal region by a large Tupi group that extends as far as Paraguay, Bolivia and part of Argentina – to form *nheengatu*, the "beautiful language" or "lingua franca". Today, as with Greek and Roman, it is one of the major etymological components of Portuguese spoken in Brazil. Some examples: Paraná – a river devoid of own life that channels water from one river to another. *Paranapanema = paraná**, poor in fish. *Pirá* – fish + *urucu* (red) = *pirarucu**. *Caa* – forest + *tinga* (white or bleached) = *caatinga*, small or sparse bush where light penetrates (not to be confused with *catinga*, probably of African origin, which means a disagreeable smell). *Canarana – cana + rana*, that which resembles = a grass similar to, but not, sugar cane. Brazilians use thousands of words without being aware of their indigenous ethnic etymological source.

Urucu – (*Bixa orellana* – from the Tupi *uru'ku* = red). The fruit of the *urucuzeiro*. A red dye can be extracted by adding a little water to the seeds of the *urucu*. This dye is widely used by the Indians to paint the body for war, for the hunt, or for festivals. It is the raw material for the red food coloring and condiment known as *colorau*.

Uxi-coroa – (*Duckesia verrucosa*). A large tree that yields edible oily fruit. We believe this refers to the *uxicuruá* recorded in official lexicons. The pronunciation of *uxi-coroa* was taken from the mid-Amazon region, in contrast to the *uxi-liso*, another fruit, similar to the *oiti*, coming from the northeastern region but also common in other regions such as Rio de Janeiro.

Várzea – The strip of land between the river and the high ground (water meadow). The lower *várzeas* are normally flooded every year while the higher *várzeas* are only submerged by heavier floods.

Vazante – The period during which the rivers have the smallest volume of water. In the Amazon region, the water level normally begins to fall in June and starts to rise again as of November or December.

Vitória-régia – (*Victoria amazonica* - Giant water lily). An aquatic plant of the Ninfeacea family whose enormous leaves can reach 1.8 meters in diameter and whose white or pink flowers (one on each plant) can reach 0.3 meters in diameter. The flowers open at night and close at the first rays of dawn.

Films used to produce the photos published in this book:
Fujichrome Velvia 50 and Provia 100

Photolithography: Ponto&Meio de Comunicação
Printing and Finishing: Oceano Indústria Gráfica